We live in a season of c ... ltural acceptance of men who p ... on in sports. Femininity has su ... ption often makes its way into t ... time where a book on biblical ... Chris Mueller does a fantastic j ... garding the design for the woman and God's purpose for the woman within the marriage relationship. May this accessible volume bring encouragement to the women in your life and within your local church.

Dr. Josh Buice, Pastor of Pray's Mill Baptist Church
Founder and President of G3 Ministries.

I have greatly benefited from Chris Mueller's ministry at Grace Community Church, as he taught my two daughters through their formative Junior and High School years. Later, while conducting women's conferences at his churches in Spokane and Phoenix, I can continue to testify to the biblical integrity of Chris' teaching.

In His Word, God gives clear guidance for the roles and responsibilities of His women. Knowing Chris and his desire to stay true to Scripture, *Let the Women Be Women* will give a clear and true portrayal of the role of God's women. Even the title suggests that Christian women are eager and ready to hear and respond to God's design for their lives.

Elizabeth George, Bestselling Author
Women's Conference Speaker

"What women these Christians have!" exclaimed Libanius, the fourth-century teacher. The Christian woman is a breed apart. In character, conduct, and commitments, she astounds and confounds the world. The Christian woman understands what the world does not, that any definition of what it means to be a woman must start with the Creator and His commandments. In this wonderful book Chris Mueller outlines God's design for women in the home, the church, and the world. Here is a timely reminder that the best thing a woman can be, is what God made her to be. Let women be women of God. Heaven will cheer, hell will mourn, and the world will sit up and take notice.

Philip De Courcy, Senior Pastor, Kindred Community Church
Teacher, Know The Truth

I first met Chris Mueller 39 years ago, as he was my college pastor at Grace Community Church. He taught a Sunday series called *Let the Women Be Women.* I had never heard such teaching before that was so biblical and needed for collegians. I still remember those foundational truths today and am thrilled that these lessons have now made their way into print! With solid exposition through the book of Titus and practical application for today, this is a must read for any young woman who desires to grow and mature in Christ.

Dr. Benjamin Shin, Associate Professor, Talbot School of Theology

In a time when every voice in our culture rages against biblical truth, Chris uncompromisingly teaches it. I am a pastor and father of four daughters who I pray will embrace the principles of biblical womanhood laid out in this book. Of course, you may not agree with every application made, but as God has promised, you will be set free by embracing the truth taught from His Word. I highly recommend this book.

Bobby Scott, Pastor, Community of Faith Bible Church

Writing to women about male-female distinctions and calling readers to reject their culture's expectations for their Creator's design may not be an enviable task, but it desperately needs to be done. After thoughtfully reading this book, many will end up thanking Pastor Chris Mueller. Here you will find timely truths from God's Word on a variety of practical topics related to womanhood, presented in a loving and forthright manner.

Dr. Mike Fabarez, President, Compass Bible Institute, Focal Point Ministries

Few concepts are more misunderstood and ill-defined than femininity. Feminism has become conflated, resulting in confusing consternation for what it means to be genuinely, biblically, and wonderfully feminine. *Let the Women Be Women* was heard in its preached form when I (Kim) was in college, and it grounded my convictions on what it looks like to be a woman pleasing to God among women actively seeking to elevate themselves above an anemic form of womanhood. Mueller clearly explains God's design for the women He created. This is a curriculum our church welcomes.

Rick Holland, Senior Pastor, Mission Road Bible Church
Kim Holland – Wife, Mother, Co-laborer

The current cultural crisis regarding gender and sexual identity necessitates the fearless proclamation of biblical truth regarding womanhood. Chris Mueller's messages were tremendously impactful during our college years. They provided a strong foundation that was not just theory but truth put into practice. This book centralizes on the authority and sufficiency of God's Word as He is the One who designed and created what it means to be a woman. This important discipleship resource is a much needed tool to raise up the next generations of godly women for God's glory.

John Kim, Senior Pastor, Lighthouse Bible Church Los Angeles
Angela Kim – Wife, Mother, Co-laborer

King Lemuel dedicated an entire chapter in God's Holy Word to the oracles his mother taught him in Proverbs 31. Toward the end of that masterful description is a stunning statement to ponder: "Charm is deceitful, and beauty is vain, but a woman who fears Yahweh, she shall be praised."
Let the Women Be Women by Chris Mueller describes the role of a godly woman in the home, church, and society from the pages of Scripture. In a confusing culture, here is a clear word on how a woman can please God.

Dr. Scott Ardavanis, Senior Pastor, Grace Church of the Valley

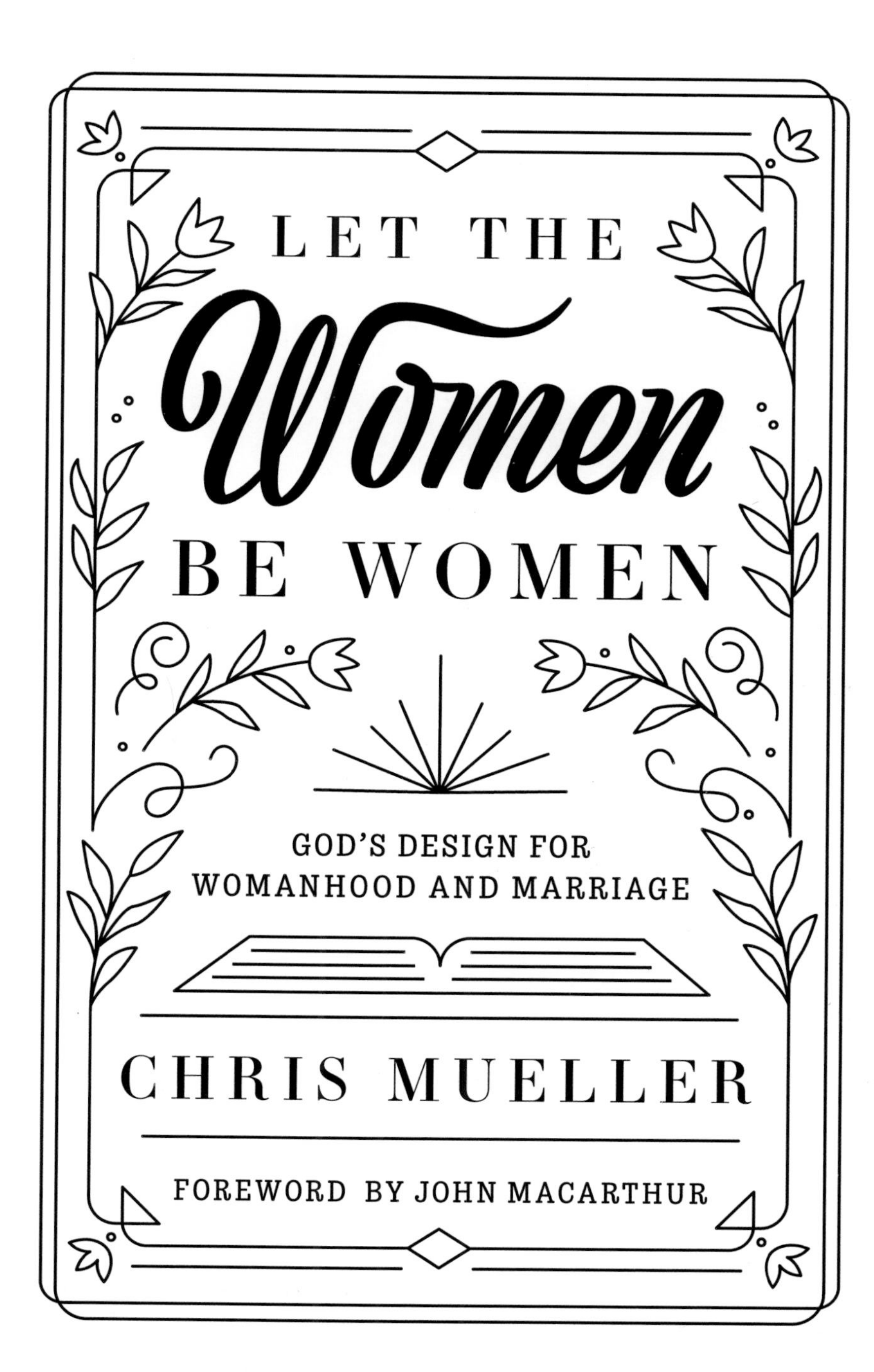

LET THE *Women* BE WOMEN

GOD'S DESIGN FOR WOMANHOOD AND MARRIAGE

CHRIS MUELLER

FOREWORD BY JOHN MACARTHUR

316publishing.com

Printed in the United States of America
26 25 24 23 22 / 1 2 3 4 5

ISBN: 978-1-63664-122-5

DEDICATION

To Jean Mueller,
next to Christ, my greatest love
and an amazing example of a godly wife, mother and grandmother;
along with the Titus 2 women
who I have had the joy of serving Christ with since 1974,
I dedicate this book.

ACKNOWLEDGEMENTS

I want to acknowledge my friends John and Patricia MacArthur
who more than any other, shaped my preaching, pastoring and marriage.

To the Elders of Faith Bible Church Murrieta
who are being used of God to shepherd the most amazing local church.

To the Congregation of Faith Bible Church Murrieta
for your constant love, encouragement, and walking in the truth.

To the Godly Women of Faith Bible Church and the Graduates of the Titus 2 Training Center Express, for your desire to be trained so that you may impact future generations of women for Christ.

To my long-term friends, couples, pastors and their wives
who are ongoing examples of these truths to the Glory of God.

To the Master's Seminary faculty and students
for being consistently biblical, and like myself,
passionately desiring to impact this world for Christ.

To Gary Kim, a collegian, who experienced the exposition of Titus 2 on men and women, and now as a publisher, lovingly pressed me to write this book and its partner book, *Let the Men Be Men.*

To Chris Scotti and other editors, along with several members of FBC
for excellent editing and encouragement
in the process of writing and refining *Let the Women Be Women.*

TABLE OF CONTENTS

FOREWORD

BY JOHN MACARTHUR

PASTOR OF GRACE COMMUNITY CHURCH IN SUN VALLEY, CALIFORNIA

CHANCELLOR OF THE MASTER'S UNIVERSITY AND SEMINARY

PRESIDENT OF GRACE TO YOU

In Proverbs 31:30, the author states that "a woman who fears Yahweh, she shall be praised." In our current times that is a challenging goal for young Christian women to achieve. The good news is that, in the book of Titus, God provides us with direct instruction on how to achieve that goal. There, the apostle Paul reveals God's clear design for how young women are to walk worthy of Jesus Christ.

I have known Chris Mueller as a friend and fellow pastor for decades. He also served alongside me at Grace Community Church for a decade before God called him to shepherd Faith Bible Church. It was during his ministry here as Grace Church's College Pastor that he originated a series from Titus called *Let the Men Be Men* and *Let the Women Be Women*. During this period our college students experienced incredible growth, both in numbers and spiritual maturity. I would know; most of my own children were blessed to be a part of this very ministry.

I am grateful that the content of that series, which Chris has continued to teach for several decades, is now published. In every generation, Christian men and women desperately need a biblical foundation on the roles which God designed, yet few churches give it. This book and its partner, *Let the Men Be Men*, are therefore all the more valuable to meet that need. If you are a young woman, or have influence on young women, you need to absorb the truth in this book for your own sake and those you impact. If you are a young man, you need to read this book to know what godly character qualities you should be looking for in a future wife. Certainly, young married women will benefit from the principles contained in *Let the Women Be Women*, since these principles are the pillars of a healthy marriage. And if you are already a mature believer, the biblical instruction in this book will refresh your pursuit of God's design for blessing and allow you to take a spiritual inventory of how you are fulfilling God's design for godly living.

While the challenges for young Christians can seem overwhelming in our current culture, God, through His Word, provides the wisdom and the power to live a life worthy of Him. I pray that this treasure of practical truth will be an encouragement to Christian young women who are fighting daily to live for our Savior's glory. And for those who are not in Christ, I hope divine instruction will awaken them to their need of the Savior to empower them, through His Spirit, to become "a woman who fears Yahweh."

INTRODUCTION

LET THE WOMEN BE WOMEN: DISCOVERING THE NEED FOR MODELING AND INSTRUCTION

Charm is deceitful and beauty is vain,
But a woman who fears Yahweh, she shall be praised.
PROVERBS 31:30

In 1983, I was redirected from leading youth ministry to become the college pastor at Grace Community Church. The college group was in trouble and the elders trusted my leadership, so they asked me to step into a ministry that had lost its way. I was 27 years old, newly married and wondering how I could turn this ministry around.

To my surprise, the 150 collegians were hungry for sound doctrine, practical theology and pastoral leadership. I started training leaders to lead Bible studies in the future. We started dreaming about starting campus Bible studies at UCLA, USC, Cal State Northridge and other nearby schools, with the goal of reaching the lost.

I started teaching on the theology of servanthood, spiritual gifts and the role every Christian has in the local church. I quickly saw collegians jump into various forms of ministry. We held garage sales to raise money for short-term missions, cleaned church properties, ministered to widows and those with disabilities. Within a couple of years, collegians were serving in almost every ministry at Grace Church.

Next, I focused on Christ's Great Commission of making disciples. I sought to define discipleship biblically as intentional relationships for the purpose of sharing the gospel and spiritual growth. Not only did I want our collegians to disciple within our group, but it was critical for the future as many would marry and one day become parents. Parenting is a form of discipleship, so getting them ready to lead the next generation was crucial.

My time with the collegians was also a lot of fun. We laughed together, cared for one another, and enjoyed great times of fellowship. Together, my wife and I watched the Lord do amazing things. The gospel was being preached and collegians were getting saved!

As I got to know these collegians, I noticed a glaring need. Women thought being a godly woman meant they must be a ministry speaker, write books and hit the Bible teaching circuit. Others were pursuing careers in business or some other field, but rarely was marriage or a family mentioned as part of their future plans. The men had a similar misunderstanding. They all believed that the only way to become a godly man was to become a pastor or missionary. There was no mention of character, spiritual leadership, or becoming a husband and father. I realized I had to do something, but had no idea what to do.

As our campus ministries were developing, I did not have enough trained staff to minister at our seven campuses. So I looked for young married couples at Grace Church who loved Christ, held to sound doctrine and could disciple collegians. As these couples started serving in our ministry, their living examples provided a picture of what a godly (not perfect) marriage looked like and the collegians (especially those coming from broken homes) were attracted to Christ and marriage because of their example.

I realized that these collegians needed to hear what God's Word says about the roles of men and women, then see God's design modeled. I started a preaching series called, *Let the Men Be Men* and *Let the Women Be Women* from Titus 2:4-8. This series rocked my world and further transformed the college ministry. The ministry grew in size, but more importantly, the students (youth to young marrieds) repented and turned to Christ.

It was incredible to see God do amazing things through the teaching of His Word. Since the 1980's, God has continued to use these messages to transform lives. Gone are the days of cassette tapes, but God's truth lives on through the free downloads available on our church's website (www.faith-bible.net).

As our world moves to greater confusion and many churches fail to teach God's Word as written, the content of these books will feel more foreign to modern readers. Regardless, the goal is to honor GOD'S DESIGN for both men and women and allow the reader to wrestle with how to obey God's Word in the midst of a distorted world.

The greatest burden some readers will struggle with is the overwhelming sense that they can't live these truths. And it is true, you and I will not be able to live God's design for men or for women unless we have been born again. And as a Christian, we can't live out God's design for a man or woman, unless we are dependent upon the Holy Spirit. Many people understand they stand condemned before a Holy God because of their sin. Therefore, they deserve to be punished forever in hell. But the merciful Father, sent His perfect Son to pay the wages of sin (which is death). Jesus Christ lived a perfect life, then offered Himself as our substitute needed to take the punishment we deserve for our sins. Christ rose from the dead, ascended into heaven and is the only One who can provide a way for you to be right with God. You must trust completely in the work of Christ by faith and turn from your sin in repentance to be saved. That is the doctrine of justification. Along with being justified, if you are a genuine Christian, you will also be regenerated. A true believer is a new creation. You look the same on the outside, but you are not the same on the inside. God gives you a new heart that wants to obey His Word.

And this is the only way any believer can ever obey God's Word and live out God's design for men and women. No one can grow to be a godly woman or godly man who doesn't have Christ indwelling them and living through them in genuine salvation. Only genuine Christians have the Spirit of God empowering them to grow into God's man or God's woman in sanctification. As you begin to read this study of God's design for women, first make certain you are truly His child. I guarantee that the challenge for women, to FEAR YAHWEH, is impossible if you walk this journey alone. Christ dwelling in you is your only hope.

1

LET THE WOMEN BE WOMEN

CUTTING THROUGH THE CONFUSION

"And God created man in His own image, in the image of God He created him; male and female He created them."

GENESIS 1:27

While playing near his easy chair, the little girl climbed up into her father's lap and stared into his face. As she felt the stubble of his beard and the wrinkles of his forehead with her soft little hands, she inquired of her father, "Did God make you, Daddy?" "Yes honey, He did make me." Then, looking at herself in a mirror on the wall across the room, she asked, "Did God make me?" He replied, "Of course honey." After a little thought, she exclaimed, "God sure seems to be doing better work lately!"

Women are a wonderful creation of God! God has a fantastic design for women that was intended from the very beginning. Yet so much of what God intended is lost in today's radical feminism, lesbianism, female preachers and lady elders, creating confusion for women who want to know exactly what God designed for them.

The goal of this book is to help reveal what the Bible says about God's design for women.

CAUSES OF CONFUSION

I believe there are five foundational reasons why there is such confusion about true femininity and masculinity within the church.

"...there are five foundational reasons why there is such confusion about true femininity and masculinity within the church."

The first reason is our society's push toward a unisex or no-sex ideal. The unisex ideal, born out of the women's liberation movement, attempts to break down all gender distinctions to the point that one's sex—female or male—is completely irrelevant. While the women's liberation movement has had some positive impact ensuring dignity and equal rights for women, many areas of this movement depart from or directly contradict what God has laid out in Scripture.

The second reason for the confusion regarding femininity and masculinity is the LGBTQ+ movement. As Christians who believe the Bible is God's Word, we understand that homosexuality and transgenderism are not a part of God's design for women and men. But its pervasiveness in our culture can influence our thinking and worldview in ways we may not realize.

The implications of these two significant movements present more challenges. While the women's liberation movement argues that one's sexual makeup shouldn't make any difference in how

"...our culture can influence our thinking and worldview in ways we may not realize."

one lives, the LGBTQ+ movement emphasizes that one's sexual makeup makes all the difference in how one lives. The world is divided not into male and female, but gay, straight, bisexual, transgender, non-binary, and a growing list of other labels. While these two movements were intended to be liberating, they have resulted in creating more complications and confusion for young women and men. Adding another layer of complexity is the ever-constant shifting of the world's standards of feminine and masculine ideals. A woman may wonder if she might be lesbian, or perhaps a man trapped in a woman's body. Or she may buy into a popular deception that there are dozens of genders.

The third reason for the confusion about gender is the breakdown of marriage. You may have experienced your parents' divorce, or may have grown up in a single-parent home. You may not have up-close experience seeing how men and women can live together in a biblical way. You may not have grown up with an admirable, godly mother or other godly role models. When we lack real-life examples, there is a greater tendency to develop our views of womanhood and manhood based on an assortment of television shows, movies, and other media. We do our best to live out our God-given gender, but without a biblical model, we are not really sure how to act, which compounds our anxiety and confusion.

The fourth reason is the distortion of gender roles paraded in social media, entertainment, news outlets, and secular education. In contrast to God's view, young women are continually bombarded with anti-biblical views on the roles of men and women. We even find these immoral ideologies embedded into kindergarten through university curriculum.

The fifth—and I think the most important—reason for confusion is that there is a significant lack of accurate, gutsy teaching of biblical truth in this area. Even in churches and institutions professing to have sound doctrine, there is an absence of true biblical instruction on how women and men are to be, based on the actual text of Scripture. This lack of boldness in unapologetically proclaiming and living out the truths of God's Word is a massive failure.

"...there is an absence of true biblical instruction on how women and men are to be, based on the actual text of Scripture."

EXAMPLES OF CONFUSION

Where does all of this leave us? For many individuals, these messages result in a perpetual state of internal conflict. For example, you may have a conflict concerning your identity. You begin to ask questions like these: *Who am I really? What kind of person am I supposed to be? How am I supposed to act in certain situations?*

The questions women wrestle with may include: *Should I pursue a career or wait to be married? Should I study more and pursue advanced degrees or focus on becoming a wife and mother? Do I try to let the guy lead, or should I tell him when he's acting like a fool?* These are all difficult questions this book will deal with.

"...if we don't really know who we're supposed to be as individuals, we can't possibly know how to interact properly with the opposite sex."

The conflict is also seen in our relationships with the opposite sex. In fact, if we don't really know who we're supposed to be as individuals, we can't possibly know how to interact properly with the opposite sex. If you have experienced that confusion in your own life, please know that you are not alone.

In my 40+ years of pastoral ministry, I can say there is nothing new under the sun. In fact what you might be confused about regarding what it means to be a woman is something that has been prevalent in our culture for decades.

THE WAY OUT OF CONFUSION

Over the years, my view of what I am supposed to be as a man before God has come into sharper focus. My understanding of biblical womanhood has become clearer as well. It may seem atypical for a man to write a book for women, but as a pastor-teacher, it is my role to teach God's Word as it is written. This book does not offer a man's perspective on what a woman is and should do, but unfolds God's design for young women. I have no desire to impose my own opinions on the reader of this book; nor do I want to imitate the thinking of a declining culture. My hope is to explain and apply God's perfect Word to all believers, both women and men.

As a younger man, I pastored over three thousand young adults in a large church. Then for the subsequent three decades I was involved in ministering to thousands more as the teaching pastor of another church as I preached the Word, counseled families, and shepherded the flock. Through all those years, I have found that the vast majority of young Christian women, from high school students to young marrieds, struggle in some way over what God designed women to do and be.

As I approach this task, my first goal is to "accurately handle" the text of Scripture (2 Tim. 2:15) and then to practically apply it. Be warned: though God's perfect Word will reveal His perfect will, God's will is often a far cry from what the world defines and dictates for women. This book will contain truth that may be difficult to hear; some things that are strange to the ear of the modern Christian and ignored by the great majority of churches in our world. The world has increasingly proven it has no clue about what God has beautifully designed for men and women. Even when it is understood, God's design is often mocked even by those who claim to be Christians.

"...God's will is often a far cry from what the world defines and dictates for women."

To really understand what God's Word says, we have to turn a deaf ear to culture, traditions and people's opinions, and work hard at determining what God meant by what He said through the biblical authors. I ask you in advance to look hard at your Bible to determine whether you have bought into human opinions or whether you are basing your beliefs on divine revelation. As a young woman, are you genuinely following God's blueprint for women?

There are very few young women today who don't struggle

"There are very few young women today who don't struggle (at least a little) with the Bible's instruction on women."

(at least a little) with the Bible's instruction on women. There are some singles who wonder if God would be more pleased with them if they gave themselves to ministry or missions and forgot about their desire for a family. Other women wonder how they can possibly apply these truths while they're going to school or pursuing a career. There are still others who wonder if these exhortations were intended to be cultural and therefore not applicable to today's liberated women.

For women to know the empowerment of God's indwelling Spirit of truth, they must obey the truth. For a Christian marriage to experience God's blessing, it must follow God's blueprint. For parents to raise girls to be godly women they must know the plan God designed. And for a woman to know what kind of man God intends for her to marry, she must know what it means to find a truly biblical man. We must take our cues from Scripture. Too many young women are looking outside of God's prescribed plan and turning to the culture's and social media's definition of womanhood.

For all believers, the focus should be to learn and live out the Word of God. Does that describe you? Do you daily meditate on His Word? Could you teach a child about the Trinity? Can you help your friends with what the Bible says about divorce? Are you ready to live by the truth and not tradition?

If you want to grow, you will not only need to learn what God's Word says but must also be a doer of the Word. You will have to learn from older godly women. Ask yourself, do you model your life after someone who is older and more mature in her Christian life than you are? I'm not talking about discipleship, though that is essential. I'm simply talking about modeling. Who do you watch? Does she provide the right example? And are you ready to imitate her lifestyle?

"Do you model your life after someone who is older and more mature in her Christian life than you are?"

GOOD NEWS!

If you're feeling overwhelmed already at the beginning of this book, I have good news for you. The biblical instruction in this book is not a list of rules to obey or commands to follow in your own strength. It's not merely about "being a better woman." Rather, all Scripture is grounded in the person and work of Jesus Christ and the power of the Holy Spirit.

In Chapter 2 of Titus we read,

> *For the grace of God has appeared, bringing salvation to all men, instructing us that, denying ungodliness and worldly desires, we should live sensibly, righteously and godly in the present age, looking for the blessed hope and the appearing of the glory of our great God and Savior, Jesus Christ, who gave Himself for us that He might redeem us from all lawlessness, and purify for Himself a people for His own possession, zealous for good works (vv. 11–14).*

And likewise, in Titus 3:

> *For we ourselves also once were foolish, disobedient, deceived, enslaved to various lusts and pleasures, spending our life in malice and envy, despicable, hating one another. But when the kindness and affection of God our Savior appeared, He saved us, not by works which we did in righteousness, but according to His mercy, through the washing of regeneration and renewing by the Holy Spirit, whom He poured out upon us richly through Jesus Christ our Savior, so that having been justified by His grace, we would become heirs according to the hope of eternal life (vv. 3–7).*

These passages are packed with the grace, mercy and love of God for His people. The Father is the architect of our salvation. The Son secures our salvation through His perfectly righteous life and substitutionary death on our behalf. The Holy Spirit empowers us to turn from sin and emulate our righteous Savior. And as born again believers, our ultimate hope is the return of Christ and to be with Him in the new heavens and new earth.

We can only embark on this journey of learning what God says about womanhood once we have experienced the stunning grace of God and the beauty of the person of Jesus Christ. We want to learn to become more like Him so that He receives honor and praise through our lives. For any young woman, there is no greater life-long journey than to diligently pursue God's design for women.

FOR PERSONAL REFLECTION & GROUP DISCUSSION:

1. Describe the kind of woman that you want to be in the future.

2. Describe the kind of woman you think God wants you to be.

3. How are your answers to the first two questions similar, and how are they different? Regarding the similarities, how do you think you can become that kind of woman? Regarding the differences, what goals do you need to change or re-prioritize?

4. What questions do you have about women's or men's roles?

5. Do you need to come to Christ for salvation? Are you in Christ and pursuing sanctification? How do you know which one you are?

6. Are you one who needs to come to Christ in salvation, or one who needs to become like Christ in sanctification? How do you know which one you are?

2

LET THE WOMEN BE BIBLICAL

GOD'S DESIGN THROUGH SCRIPTURE

"All Scripture is God-breathed and profitable for teaching, for reproof, for correction, for training in righteousness..."

2 TIMOTHY 3:16

You may be wondering, ***what's this guy's attitude toward women?*** I like them, especially my wife Jean! In our 40+ years of marriage, we still seek to follow the Scriptures and pursue God's design together. We both believe obeying God's Word results in great blessing. That blessing is based upon the truth that God designed only two sexes, male and female, each with a specific role. The joy of God's design also includes a clear awareness that men need women and women need men. No man could be here without a woman and no woman could be here without a man—we need each other!

I am neither a chauvinist nor a feminist. I think both of these positions are wrong. I am a biblicist. I don't care what the popular opinion of our day is on any issue—all I really care about is what the Bible says. I take the Bible literally. Discovering our Creator's perfect will for women and men comes only from a correct understanding of the Scriptures. To know what God meant by what God said in His Word, you must interpret the Bible by asking, *what did the author intend to say to the original audience he wrote?* In other words, we must pursue a normal interpretation of the Bible.

Titus 2:3-5 will provide most of our answers, but not all of them. This passage is only part of the picture. It is essential for you to see that the entire Scripture, from Genesis to Revelation, extols God's design for women. This chapter will give you a taste of what the Bible teaches about God's design for women and it will prove the consistency of God's plan. Our Lord is the one who created us; we would be foolish to ignore His perfect plan for women and men.

"It is essential for you to see that the entire Scripture, from Genesis to Revelation, extols God's design for women."

GOD'S VIEW OF WOMEN FROM THE BEGINNING

The overall teaching of Scripture is that men and women are equal before the Lord but their responsibilities are different. In Genesis, we see both the woman's equality of being and also her responsibility of submission.

> *God created man in His own image, in the image of God He created him; male and female He created them. God blessed them, and God said to them, "Be*

fruitful and multiply, and fill the earth, and subdue it;" (Genesis 1:27-28)

Here is the equality of being. Man and woman are equally created in the image of God. Now consider their roles and how the fall affected things.

"Both man and woman were created in the image of God. Neither received more of God's image than the other."

BEFORE THE FALL

Both man and woman were created in the image of God. Neither received more of God's image than the other. God gave the command to multiply and subdue the earth to both the man and the woman. In these aspects of creation, the two are equals.

Even though man was created first, he wasn't complete on his own.

Then Yahweh God said, "It is not good for the man to be alone; I will make him a helper suitable for him." And out of the ground Yahweh God had formed every beast of the field and every bird of the sky, and He brought each to the man to see what he would call it; and whatever the man called a living creature, that was its name. And the man gave names to all the cattle and to the birds of the sky and to every beast of the field; but for Adam there was not found a helper suitable for him. (Genesis 2:18-20)

"...God made woman, the perfect helper for Adam."

God showed the animals to Adam to expose his need. There would be many animals to help him, but none that could be his life companion, his soul mate. Instead, God made woman, the perfect helper for Adam.

> *So Yahweh God caused a deep sleep to fall upon the man, and he slept; then He took one of his ribs and closed up the flesh at that place. And Yahweh God fashioned the rib, which He had taken from the man, into a woman, and He brought her to the man. Then the man said,*
> *"This one finally is bone of my bones,*
> *And flesh of my flesh;*
> *This one shall be called Woman,*
> *Because this one was taken out of Man."*
> *Therefore a man shall leave his father and his mother, and cleave to his wife; and they shall become one flesh. And the man and his wife were both naked and were not ashamed. (Genesis 2:21-25)*

God created Adam, and for a short time he was the only human on earth. God pronounced Adam's aloneness as "not good," emphasizing the need to create a partner "suitable" for him, or one "corresponding to" him. God's second human creation was Eve, and she was brought forth from Adam's body rather than being created independently, as he had been. Why? To show them their dependence and need for each other. The purpose of creating the woman was for the man. Eve was created to be a helper for Adam.

She was created to be suitable for the man, and Genesis 2:24 tells us that God's plan was for them to be one flesh.

AFTER THE FALL

Genesis 3 describes the fall of mankind into sin. The woman was created to be a helper to the man and thus submit to his leadership. But Eve took the lead when the serpent tempted her, and she made a wrong decision without consulting Adam.

As a result, God cursed Adam, Eve, and the serpent. And from that time, mankind has been sinful to the core, totally depraved, unable to respond to God on our own and in need of salvation. There were other long-lasting consequences women must deal with because of Adam and Eve's failure. Genesis 3:16 reads, "To the woman He said, 'I will greatly multiply your pain and conception, in pain you will bear children; your desire will be for your husband, and he will rule over you.'"

We see that the curse upon Eve resulted in three serious consequences:

1. "in pain you will bear children"
2. "your desire will be for your husband"
3. "he will rule over you"

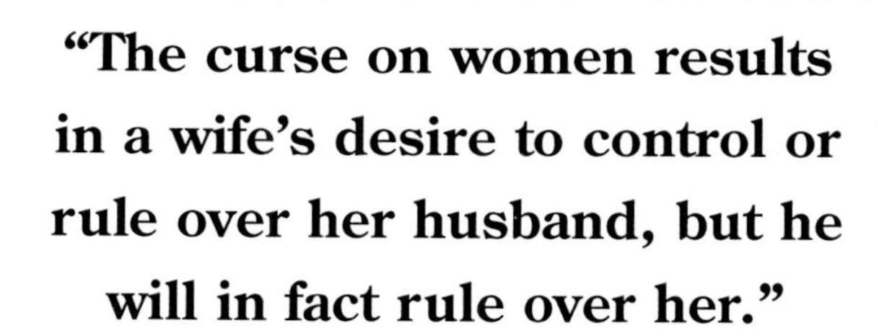

The same Hebrew word translated "desire" in Genesis 3:16 is also used in Genesis 4:7 with the obvious meaning of a desire to control: "Sin is lying at the door; and its desire is for you, but you must rule over it." The curse on women results in a wife's desire to control or rule over her husband, but he will in fact rule over her. This is the source of much marital conflict and one of the biggest stressors in other male-female relationships.

AFTER THE CROSS

The actions of men toward women throughout history have often been harsh and abusive. Too many men have used the Bible to excuse their unacceptable treatment of women. Some believe that the submission of wives to husbands is not found in the creation account, but is solely the result of the fall and the curse. Therefore, they believe that through salvation in Christ, Christians today have overcome the curse and returned to an ideal equality of roles that they believe existed at creation.

However, a careful study of Genesis 2 before the fall shows that the submission of the woman was present at creation because she was created for the purpose of being Adam's helper. Paul affirms this by using Genesis 2 as a foundation to instruct women on submission in marriage. (See 1 Corinthians 11:8-12, 1 Timothy 2:11-13). Submission is not a result of the fall, and salvation in Christ does not undo the principle of submission, whether it be the submission of children to parents, citizens to the government, employees to their bosses, church members to their leaders, or wives to their husbands.

Salvation in Christ does not wipe out all effects of the fall, like pain in childbirth. When a husband and wife are born again and obeying God's perfect design, they both will understand how submission returns the blessings of harmony and oneness that their Creator originally intended.

Sadly, our culture has turned submission into a negative concept, and many believers have a misunderstanding of how submission actually works in marriage. The key is to look to God Himself. God is one, yet He is also three distinct persons—Father, Son and Holy Spirit. All three Persons of the Trinity are equally and fully God, yet they function in different roles. After the incarnation, when Jesus lived and ministered on earth, He lived in submission to the Father. He was not less than God, He was fully God. Yet He demonstrated submission to the Father. In the same way, God's design includes the submission of a wife to her own husband—not to all men.

"To say, think, or even feel that submission makes women inferior would be to say that Jesus is inferior to the Father— and that is heresy.

To say, think, or even feel that submission makes women inferior would be to say that Jesus is inferior to the Father—and that is heresy. Our Lord modeled submission, just as 1 Corinthians 11:3 teaches, "I want you to understand that Christ is the head of every man, and the man is the head of a woman, and God is the head of Christ." There will be more explanation on this in chapter 10 but for now, don't be turned off by God's design of submission—it is a beautiful way to imitate Christ and glorify God.

Fallen men have abused their role repeatedly throughout history which contributes to many women reacting negatively toward the idea of submission. However, a born again believer should embrace the biblical concept of submission. Why? As mentioned before, the Bible tells believers they are to submit to parents, to employers, to secular authorities, to law enforcement officials, to your church leadership, to God, to Christ, to the Word of God and to one another (the passages will be listed later). The point is, Christians are called to submit to authority in every walk of life. And in the marriage relationship, a wife is called on by God to submit to her husband. Her husband is the head in their marriage relationship, as God is the head of Christ. This is not because the husband is better, but because this is God's design.

Unfortunately, because submission can be a stumbling block for women, they often don't realize the amazing role that God has given them to pursue. The vast majority of all ministry to women in the church is to be done by women. In fact, in the New Testament, God's design is that men minister to men and women minister to women. Women teach women, reach women, and minister to the needs of other women.

The Bible shows that there are women who functioned as patrons. For example, in Luke 8:2-3, Jesus' disciples included some women who helped pay the bills for His ministry. Others opened their homes, like Lydia in Acts 16:14-15. Many women worked hard in the process of ministry (Romans 16:6, 12). Others were faithful evangelists (Philippians 4:2-3). Some were merciful caregivers (Mark 15:40-41). In Titus 2, godly older women are instructed to be the primary trainers of younger women.

That is just some of what women can do, are called to do and have always been doing for the glory of God in the church of Christ. So don't allow submission to taint your view of women, especially since our Lord Jesus Christ also submitted to the Father (1 Corinthians 11:3).

Do not allow God's design for women to be corrupted in your thinking. Remember, it is only because of sin that such corruption has occurred. In their fallen sinfulness, both men and women began to malign and deviate from God's perfect design for women. Both sexes lost sight of God's design that the two would become one. That is why we first must be restored to a right relationship with God through Christ, and then follow the Word of God as our only pattern to discover God's perfect design for women and for marriage. The Old and New Testaments give detailed instructions for how believers are to enjoy and respect both sexes.

GOD'S VIEW OF WOMEN IN THE NEW TESTAMENT

Something that most people don't realize is that the abuse of women was rampant in the first-century Greek and Roman cultures. However, Jesus demonstrated something totally different. Be encouraged by these examples of Jesus love and care for women:

- In John 4:7-38, Jesus speaks publicly to the Samaritan woman and treats her with respect, which amazes the disciples.
- In Luke 8:2-3, a band of women travel with Jesus and minister to Him and His disciples.
- In Luke 10:38-39, we find that Jesus had close friends who were women.
- In Luke 7:44, Jesus publicly affirms a woman in front of men.
- In Luke 8:43-48, Jesus breaks religious taboos about ritual uncleanness in women by touching the woman with the menstrual problem.
- In Matthew 27:55, women are the last to leave the site of the crucifixion.
- In Mark 16:1, women are the first at the tomb.
- In John 20:14, Jesus first appears to women after His resurrection and commissions them as the first witnesses to the good news.

Notice how revolutionary Christianity was to the culture. "There is neither Jew nor Greek, there is neither slave nor free man, there is no male and female, for you are all one in Christ Jesus." (Galatians 3:28) In this verse, Paul is not talking about male and female roles but our equal standing before God, found in Jesus Christ alone. There is no difference between men or women in our standing before God, because of Christ. The roles of men and women are different, but their standing is exactly the same. This was God's design from the very beginning and Jesus made it clear in what He taught about women and how He treated them. In His ministry, Christ brought a freedom to women they had not experienced in the culture at that time. Christ also brought freedom and respect to men, slaves and Gentiles that they had never known. So how should a Christian woman act?

THE ROLE OF A WOMAN TO HER HUSBAND

Survey the New Testament and you will not only discover what God designed for women, but also find God's instruction toward women very consistent. Yet, as a believer, you must remember that even though it might be simple to understand the truth, it is not easy to live it. No one instantly becomes a godly wife on her wedding day. Most of what the Bible says to married women also applies to single women—in fact, these biblical commands and principles are what single women are to pursue before they get married.

"Growing into a God-pleasing woman and living out His design takes time!"

Growing into a God-pleasing woman and living out His design takes time! It never happens in a day, or by a single decision, or through a conference or even by reading a book. But God will make it happen as He completes what He has started in your life (Philippians 1:6). Even though God is sovereign you are responsible to dependently obey His Word through the power of the indwelling Holy Spirit.

Ephesians 5:22-33 is the lengthiest New Testament passage about marriage. In it the apostle Paul teaches that marriage was designed to be a spiritual object lesson on Christ and His relationship to the church. When you look at a Christian marriage, you should recognize its similarity to the relationship between Jesus and His bride, the church.

- Christ is the head of the church (v. 23).

- Jesus leads the church because He loves and tenderly cares for His bride and gives Himself to meet her needs (vv. 25-27).
- Christ demonstrates His total love and unselfishness by dying for the church (v. 25b).
- The church is to submit to His loving leadership (v. 24a).

"When you look at a Christian marriage, you should recognize its similarity to the relationship between Jesus and His bride, the church."

Each point has implications for husbands and wives and reveals important foundational truth about God's design for marriage.

- The husband is the spiritual leader of his wife—not because he is smarter or superior, but because this mirrors God's own Person and character (v. 23).
- Like Christ, the husband is to lead his wife by loving her and serving her—and this will only occur when he dies to self and sacrifices for his wife as his greatest love next to Christ (vv. 28-29).
- Like Christ, the husband's love must be such that he would be willing to make the ultimate sacrifice and die for his wife (v. 25).
- Like the church, the wife is to submit to her husband's leadership and respect him (vv. 22, 33).

Look carefully at what God expects of husbands and wives. If your future husband truly treated you like Christ treats the church, how many of you would have a problem submitting to his leadership?

Headship within a Christian marriage is God's design because there cannot be two leaders. Submission is not always easy, but it is what the Lord commands believers to pursue. Husbands are to lead their wives with love, understanding and a willingness to die for her. The biblical concept of headship shows the world the relationship Christ has with His bride, the church.

Colossians 3:18 teaches the same truth, "Wives, be subject to your husbands, as is fitting in the Lord." The word "subject" is from a military term meaning "to rank under." But why is a wife to rank herself under her husband? Paul says that submission is "fitting," which means "proper," referring to something that's legally binding. In other words, it isn't optional.

"When each actor is committed to their own part with excellence and they work in harmony, their roles bring applause from the audience."

This doesn't mean that women are inferior to men. What God has designed is like a great play in which there are two great actors of equal skill, talent, and capacity. But one actor plays the lead role and the other plays the supportive role. When each actor is committed to their own part with excellence and they work in harmony, their roles bring applause from the audience.

It's the same with husbands and wives. They perform different roles that complement, complete and create harmony if both do what God has called them to do. This type of marriage union receives God's approval.

What Paul taught is also what Peter taught because God's Word is consistent. 1 Peter 3:1-2 says, "In the same way, you wives, be subject to your own husbands so that even if any of them are disobedient to the word, they may be won without a word by the conduct of their wives, as they observe your pure conduct with fear."

Notice that the wife's submission is to her own husband in a private, intimate and unique relationship. It is true that all Christians are called to manifest a heart attitude of submission to one another out of reverence for Christ (Ephesians 5:21). But notice, in marriage, the command to submit given in 1 Peter is not for women to submit to all men, but for a wife to submit to her own husband.

THE ROLE OF A WOMAN IN THE CHURCH BODY

As we continue to consider what the Bible says about women's roles, don't forget that the biblical principles of authority and submission apply to every aspect of our lives. It applies to our relationship to the government—we're to submit to leaders and pay taxes. In the family, children are to submit to parents. In the church, we're all to submit to a team of qualified elders. All humans are called to submit to God.

When you examine what the word "ministry" means, I think you'll understand how important the role of women is to the health of a church. Ministry is serving the needs of others in the power of the Holy Spirit, for the glory of God.

In the New Testament alone, there are examples of women in ministry. Priscilla (a.k.a. Prisca) is mentioned six times in the New Testament. Then there is Lydia, Chloe, Dorcus, Euodia, Syntyche, Philip's four daughters and a whole crew of other women who were prominent in the early church.

I shudder to think what the church would do without the ministry of women. So what is it that a woman can and cannot do in the local church? As the Bible offers all we need for life and godliness (2 Peter 1:3), we must look to Scripture for clear instruction on the role of women in ministry.

Women are not to officially teach the Word of God over

men. In 1 Timothy 2:12-15 Paul describes women in the corporate worship gathering of the church.

> *But I do not allow a woman to teach or exercise authority over a man, but to remain quiet. For it was Adam who was first formed, and then Eve. And it was not Adam who was deceived, but the woman being deceived, fell into trespass. But she will be saved through the bearing of children, if they continue in faith and love and sanctification with self-restraint.*

In public, formal teaching, women are not to teach or exercise authority over men. This is because Adam was formed first and then Eve. And it was not Adam who was deceived, but Eve was deceived and fell into sin.

The differing roles exist because of the created order—God's design from the beginning. What is a woman's role, if not to be teachers of adult men? She will be saved through the bearing of children, if they continue in faith and love and sanctification with self-restraint. In most cases, a married woman has children and much of her influence for the kingdom of Christ is through raising godly children. God gives her the high privilege of discipling boys and girls to impact the kingdom of God for His glory.

Biblically, women are not to have an authoritative role in public worship or in any formal teaching environment where both men and women are present. Some people today believe that if their pastor delegates authority to a woman, it is okay for her to preach. Others believe that if a woman has the gift of teaching, she can teach anyone. Paul says otherwise because of God's character and God's design. Yes, a woman can participate by singing, sharing her testimony and participating in a Q&A or a discussion. She is not to be in a situation where she is proclaiming God's Word as the authority for all believers to a mixed audience of men and women in the capacity of a teacher or preacher.

Paul's reasoning follows the order of creation and the fall, so we know that this prohibition is not merely cultural, but God's plan designed from the beginning. This is what is best for all women at all times.

Women are not to function as Pastors or Elders. Paul goes on to explain to Timothy about elders/pastors/overseers, which are all the same office in the New Testament. 1 Timothy 3:2 says, "An overseer, then, must be above reproach, the husband of one wife." And in verses 4-5 Paul says that an overseer must be "leading his own household well, having his children in submission with all dignity (but if a man does not know how to lead his own household, how will he take care of the church of God?)" Not only are all the qualifications for the office of overseer addressed only to men, but this specific one precludes women because the New Testament clearly teaches that men, not women, are the leaders of their households (Ephesians 5:22-24, Colossians 3:18).

There is no support in the New Testament for women to teach men or to lead as pastors or elders in the church. The headship in God's larger family (the church), as in our individual households, is a role God has designed for men.

Women are to Serve in the church. The kind of women described in 1 Timothy 3:11 are often directed by elders or deacons to lead various ministries to women and children. Church history tells us that these "Titus 2 Women" typically did four things in New Testament times:

1. Took care of the sick and poor
2. Visited Christian prisoners, providing food, clothing and letters
3. Participated in baptisms, helping the women before and after being immersed
4. Generally ministered to women in need

The New Testament is very pointed that all women are to minister their gifts in the church. 1 Peter 4:10 says, "As each one [male or female] has received a gift, employ it in serving one

"...all women are to minister their gifts in the church."

another, as good stewards of the manifold grace of God." As well, 1 Corinthians 12 says this about spiritual gifts, "To each one [male and female] is given the manifestation of the Spirit for what is profitable" (v. 7) and "One and the same Spirit works all these things, distributing to each one [male and female] individually just as He wills" (v. 11). Romans 12:4-6a tells us the body of Christ is made up of many members, both male and female: "For just as we have many members in one body and all the members do not have the same function, so we, who are many, are one body in Christ, and individually members one of another, but having gifts that differ according to the grace given to us." The Holy Spirit has gifted every true Christian with a spiritual gifting to be used in service to the church. Romans 12 and 1 Corinthians 12 remind us that these gifts might include serving, teaching, exhorting, giving, showing mercy, helping, administrating and more.

THE ROLE OF A WOMAN IN HER HOME

Titus 2:4-5 spells it out clearly: older women are to "instruct the young women in sensibility: to love their husbands, to love their children, to be sensible, pure, workers at home, kind, being subject to their own husbands, so that the Word of God will not be slandered."

For a woman of God, the home is not her prison but her priority. It is where she fulfills her God ordained duty and enjoys her privileges as a wife and mother. The principle of women in the home is timeless. This is reflected in 1 Timothy 5:14 when Paul says, "I want younger widows to get married, bear children, keep house, and give the enemy no opportunity for reviling." The work required to enjoy a Godly marriage, raising children who might follow Christ, engaging in ministry in a local church and sharing the gospel with the lost can be an overwhelming duty for a wife to pursue. A wife and mother has a unique role in developing and maintaining a home which honors Christ. Her home becomes a joy to her family and a witness to the watching world. That is no simple task. The world is telling you that all those things are secondary but Christ is telling you, that next to Him, all those things are primary.

"A wife and mother has a unique role in developing and maintaining a home which honors Christ."

Godly women today will never be free from condescending looks when they answer the career question with, "I am a homemaker." At the same time, women who live by the conviction of God's Word over trends, experts, ideas and norms will experience a joy others will never know. Young women who know Christ, follow His Word and rely dependently upon the Holy Spirit, will be blessed beyond measure for pursuing the Lord's design of a home priority. The faithful wife and mother who focuses on her home believes God's principles over peer pressure. That woman will be greatly blessed. Proverbs 31:28-30 says it best,

> *Her children rise up and bless her;*
> *As for her husband, he also praises her, saying:*
> *"Many daughters have done excellently,*
> *But you have gone above them all."*
> *Charm is deceitful and beauty is vain,*
> *But a woman who fears Yahweh, she shall be praised.*

"The faithful wife and mother who focuses on her home believes God's principles over peer pressure."

Pursuing God's design for women means dealing with the heart. In her heart, a godly woman will understand that her home is a priority, and will do her work at home as much as possible. The home is the ministry base God created for her and is where she can flourish in her gifts and creativity. For the vast majority of women who pursue God's design as a wife, mother and homemaker—their hearts are satisfied and filled with joy, knowing that they are pleasing the Lord.

A godly woman's heart will be focused on her husband, children and home, not only as her priority but also as her most important identity. Anything she does outside the home will come after she takes care of the priorities of her husband, children, home, church and witness for Christ.

Some women have no choice but to work outside the home and others may choose to work as their children grow older. None of those situations will minimize their heart's priority. After her love for Christ the godly woman will seek to fulfill her role towards her husband, children, home and church. These comprise her main priorities.

Sadly the world only extols women at work; only praises women who pursue careers; and only affirms women who have an identity in anything other than as a wife and mother. Most single women today, even Christians, are embarrassed to share that they desire to invest their life in being a wife and mother. The enemy has been really effective in propagating a gender confused, feminist, anti-Christian message to the world and sadly most pulpits in churches have acquiesced to the pressure and ignore the clear teaching of Scripture. The farther away culture moves from God's Word, the more her life will be in contrast to the world. Godly wives, mothers and homemakers are increasingly asked, 'How is it that your marriage is so strong?"; "Why are your kids so well behaved?"; "Why is your home always so welcoming?"

God has told us that a woman's greatest impact for the kingdom of God will be her influence in the lives of her children (Psalm 127:3-5). That's why Paul instructs Timothy that motherhood will be a woman's "salvation" (1 Timothy 2:15). She will impact the kingdom through the discipling of her children. May God raise up more women committed to raising up godly children to impact this world for God's glory.

FOR PERSONAL REFLECTION & GROUP DISCUSSION:

1. What are some biases and fears that you bring with you into a study of women's roles?

2. Why do you think modern culture believes the concept or idea of submission is wrong?

3. Do you believe that following God's design for women will lead to abundant blessings? Why or why not?

4. How would you identify an older godly woman? Single out a character quality you would like to emulate.

5. Why do you think God places the priority of the woman in the home? What is the impact her ministry has on the world?

3

LET THE WOMEN BE DISCIPLERS

THE NECESSITY OF MENTORSHIP

"But refuse godless myths fit only for old women. On the other hand, train yourself for the purpose of godliness,..."

1 TIMOTHY 4:7

What is an older woman? One little girl wrote this:

> *A grandmother is a lady who has no children of her own, so she likes other people's little girls. Grandmas don't have to do anything except be there. They are old so they shouldn't play hard or run. It is enough if they take us to the market and buy candy. If they take us for walks, they should slow down when passing pretty leaves or caterpillars. They never say, "Hurry up." They usually wear glasses and funny underwear. They can take their teeth and gums off. When they read to us, they don't skip or mind if it's the same story again and again. Everybody should try to have one,*

because Grandmas are the only grown-ups who have time.

If that's how grandchildren view grandmas, how do grandmas view themselves? One elderly woman wrote this:

Dear Family,

I have become 65 years old since I saw you last, and a few changes have come into my life. Frankly, I have become quite a frivolous old gal. I am seeing four different gentlemen every day. As soon as I wake up, WILL POWER helps me get out of bed. Then I go to see JOHN. Then CHARLIE HORSE comes along and when he is here, he takes a lot of my time and attention. When he leaves, ARTHUR RITUS shows up and stays the rest of the day. What a life—I'm never alone!

Older women certainly have their struggles, but can you imagine a world without them? A world without grandmothers? No special treats, unexpected gifts or money, long hugs, kindness, smiles, sympathy, understanding, listening ears, gracious words or compassion.

Before Paul addresses the issue of younger women in Titus 2:4-5, he speaks to the older women who should be training those younger women. The older women are to model the priorities of God's design and train the younger women to pursue it.

For a young woman to understand God's design for her life, she must first understand the larger context of Titus and, specifically, what it says about older women. When a younger woman understands this, she will also understand what kind of woman God wants her to become. She will understand the importance of the training she is to receive from older women. This understanding provides a goal to aim for as well as some guidance for finding one or more mentors.

THE CONTEXT OF TITUS 1-2

Titus was a ministerial protégé of the apostle Paul. Many on the island had turned to Christ through the missionary efforts of Paul and others, so Paul said to Titus at the beginning of the letter, "For this reason I left you in Crete, that you would set in order what remains and appoint elders in every city as I directed you" (Titus 1:5).

We learn from Titus 1:12 and history books, that Crete was a perverse place made up of untrustworthy people. In addition, false teachers had invaded the island, injecting errant doctrinal views into the young churches.

"You must not live life like the false teachers, but you must pursue living out healthy Christ-like doctrine."

Paul charges Titus to reinforce the need for the Cretans to be genuinely saved and fully immersed in a healthy local church overseen by qualified elders. Next, Paul offers a contrast to the false teachers: "But as for you, speak the things which are proper for sound doctrine" (Titus 2:1). You must not live life like the false teachers, but you must pursue living out healthy Christ-like doctrine.

The Greek word for "sound" in "sound doctrine" means "being healthy, living well." From it we get the English word "hygiene." The Greek word is used by Jesus in Luke 5:31 when He says, "It is not those who are well who need a physician, but those who are sick." Healthy doctrine is teaching that makes you more like Christ.

This is also what Paul describes in Titus 2 when he addresses older men, then older women, younger women and younger men; he wants their doctrine to be healthy, leading to a lifestyle of Christlikeness. God's design is for older women to model and train younger women to have healthy doctrine.

What should your motive be for pursuing godliness? Is it so you can look good, check the boxes on a bunch of rules or get God to love you more? None of those! Look at Titus 2:11-12 for the answer:

> *For the grace of God has appeared, bringing salvation to all men, instructing us that, denying ungodliness and worldly desires, we should live sensibly, righteously and godly in the present age (Titus 2:11-12).*

The context of Titus 2 says that you should want to live a godly life because of all that Jesus Christ has done for you. Both older and younger women will desire a life-long pursuit of sound doctrine as an expression of their love and submission to Christ.

HOW OLD IS OLD?

You might ask, "How old is an older woman?" Paul doesn't specify what the age a woman would have to be in order to qualify for the title "older woman." The best biblical clue we have is in 1 Timothy 5:9, "A widow is to be put on the list only if she is not less than sixty years old." That definitely defines the older woman. Yet you know there are also many women who are younger than sixty who can also be exemplary models and mentors. Those who have considerable spiritual maturity, experience as obedient Christians and lots of practice in good works, can also function as great mentors. Even young single women, who are just a few years older than younger teens, can mentor junior high girls and provide a good example of godliness. Sometimes the women training you will not be much older numerically, but super helpful spiritually.

"Sometimes the women training you will not be much older numerically, but super helpful spiritually."

TRAITS OF A GODLY OLDER WOMAN

Through Paul's words to Titus, God is giving us the qualities necessary for older women to make a very special impact for His glory. "Older women likewise are to be reverent in their behavior, not malicious gossips nor enslaved to much wine, teaching what is good, so that they may instruct the young women" (Titus 2:3-4a).

LIVING IN THE PRESENCE OF GOD

God first says that older women are to be "reverent." What does that mean? This word is used only here in the New Testament, and is a combination of two Greek words.

"Reverent" means "proper for a temple" or "fitting for a sacred service." It is picturing a priestess in a temple—giving exclusive service to God, living all of life in God's presence. But Paul also adds that older women must be reverent "in their behavior." This word also means "demeanor," or "set in order," which is more than behavior and includes attitude, speech, appearance, clothing and other aspects of a woman's lifestyle.

Being reverent in your behavior and demeanor points to your habits and heart, your attitudes and appearance, your conduct and character—what people see and what they don't see. In other words, a godly older woman's entire life is set in order.

Now, put the entire phrase together and you'll see that "reverent in their behavior" means to carry into daily life the demeanor of a priestess in a temple. Approach every aspect of life as a sacred duty performed in the presence of your Lord and Savior, Jesus

Christ. Practically, "reverent in your behavior" points to several key applications.

"Approach every aspect of life as a sacred duty performed in the presence of your Lord and Savior, Jesus Christ."

First, a reverent woman doesn't divide life up into sacred and secular. As Christians we live in two worlds at once—the natural world and the spiritual world. We live on earth in this body and toil along with everyone else. As believers we also enjoy a heavenly status and have intimate fellowship with Christ. It is easy to think that only the spiritual things are important and the regular everyday matters of living are not as important. But that is a lie.

We can think that Bible study, prayer, singing and church are of higher priority—whereas things like sleep, eating, school, relationships, our job, social media, working out and other similar activities are incidental by comparison. This causes many of us to try to walk a tightrope between both worlds, with no peace in either. We are either too heavenly-minded or too focused on earthly things.

So, what's the biblical solution? Well, the first light of hope is found in Jesus Christ Himself, who was both 100% human and 100% God—two natures in one Person. He was not schizophrenic, but totally at peace. Jesus said about His Father, "I always do the things that are pleasing to Him" (John 8:29). Everything He did, all the time, pleased God.

When Jesus walked this earth He did a lot of normal activities, like eating, sleeping, traveling, cleaning up and working—all of that pleased God too. Luke 2:52 says, "Jesus was advancing in wisdom and stature, and in favor with God and men." Jesus grew in every area and everything He did was a spiritual act. Jesus pleased God with great things and with simple things, with the religious things and the normal things. God reminds all Christians to live the same way: 1 Corinthians 10:31 says, "Whether, then, you eat or drink or whatever you do, do all to the glory of God."

For an older woman to be reverent in her demeanor, she must not divide her life into spiritual things and earthly things. Every aspect of her life is intended to glorify God. She becomes a great model for the younger woman to imitate because she lives every aspect of life to please God.

Second, a reverent woman walks in the Spirit. Like the great saints of old who walked with God, the reverent woman will live out these verses: "Be filled with the Spirit" (Ephesians 5:18) and "walk by the Spirit and you will not carry out the desire of the flesh" (Galatians 5:16).

"A mature, godly woman realizes she can't live the Christian life on her own, but that Christ can live in her through the Holy Spirit."

A mature, godly woman realizes she can't live the Christian life on her own, but that Christ can live in her through the Holy Spirit. Every true Christian has the Holy Spirit indwelling them (Romans 8:9). We already have all of the Holy Spirit through salvation, but to be filled with the Spirit means that the Holy Spirit has all of us.

To be filled with the Spirit is to be constantly saturated in God's Word (Colossians 3:16). The Spirit of Truth empowers those who walk by the truth of God's Word. Being filled with the Spirit also means living moment by moment being dependent upon the Spirit, similar to a toddler learning to walk by holding her parent's hand. To be filled with the Spirit also means you confess and repent of all known sin so you don't grieve or quench the Spirit (Ephesians 4:30, 1 Thessalonians 5:19). The Holy Spirit provides gifts to each Christian (1 Corinthians 12:1-7) so that you are empowered to faithfully serve the Lord and others.

Older godly women know that in order to glorify God, they must be able to say from their hearts, "I have been crucified with Christ, and it is no longer I who live, but Christ lives in me. And the life which I now live in the flesh I live by faith in the Son of God, who loved me and gave Himself up for me" (Galatians 2:20). She will live in the presence of God with no division of sacred and secular.

A TONGUE UNDER CONTROL

Titus 2:3a adds that "Older women likewise are to be reverent in their behavior, not malicious gossips." "Malicious gossips" is actually one word in the Greek language. It is used 35 times in the NT, and 32 of those times it is translated "devil." A malicious gossip is an accusing, slandering devil and anyone who gossips is doing Satan's work. This Greek word (diabolos) is where we get our English word "diabolical."

Mature godly women are not devilish with their tongues. They do not aid the enemy by listening to or passing on gossip or slander.

Jesus said in Matthew 12:34b-35, "the mouth speaks out of that which fills the heart. The good man brings out of his good treasure what is good; and the evil man brings out of his evil treasure what is evil."

The story is told of a young woman who asked her mentor, "I've sinned by listening to and repeating slanderous statements. What should I do now?" The godly older woman replied, "Put a feather on every doorstep in town." So the woman did just that. She then came back to the godly woman wondering if there was anything else that she should do. The answer was, "Now go back and pick up all those feathers." "That's impossible," the young woman said. "By now the wind will have blown them all over town!" And the mentor replied, "So have your slanderous words become impossible to retrieve."

It's not the gossiping mouth that's the problem, but something twelve inches lower. The issue is a matter of your heart. Gossip is a big deal because it always exposes a very sick heart. It is a serious, contagious, subversive, subtle and rebellious sin and must be cut out of our lives.

"Gossip is a big deal because it always exposes a very sick heart."

NOT ADDICTED TO ANYTHING

In Titus 2:3, the second and third qualities listed are both negative: "not malicious gossips nor enslaved to much wine." Gossip is what comes out of the mouth and "much wine" is that which goes into the mouth. A mature woman is not only one who can control her tongue, but can also control her desire for 'much wine'.

I find it very interesting that Paul talks about not being enslaved to much wine. This was a problem in the first century and even today women are trying to cope with the hardships of a fallen world, including brutish, unfaithful and at times physically abusive husbands. Even women who are born again may turn to drinking to provide a false escape.

Mature Christian women refuse to allow any kind of addiction to take hold and remain unchecked in their lives. And before you begin to look down on drunkards, remember that the Lord doesn't want us to be enslaved to anything. Alcohol is not the only addiction that plagues us. Titus 3:3 says that "we ourselves also once were foolish, disobedient, deceived, enslaved to various lusts and pleasures." Paul also tells us in 1 Corinthians 6:12, "All things are lawful for me, but not all things are profitable. All things are lawful for me, but I will not be mastered by anything."

No Christian should be addicted to any form of beverage, food, drug, social media, internet usage, shopping, video game or fleshly pleasure. Mature Christians will not allow themselves to be controlled by anything that will harm their body, cloud their thinking or hinder their testimony for Jesus. Instead Christians should be controlled by the Holy Spirit and nothing else. Mature women never solve their discontentment or regrets by turning to drink or any other form of addiction.

TRAINING YOUNGER WOMEN

Paul tells us next about a major responsibility and activity of every mature Christian woman—they must be "teaching what is good, so that they may instruct the young women" (Titus 2:3-4).

"Teaching what is good" is one word in the Greek – a compound word created from two roots meaning "instructor" and "beautiful" (or "good"). It is only used here in the New Testament and refers primarily to teaching by example so that others will learn beautiful virtues, good habits, godly behavior, and right attitudes.

Why do young women need training from older women?

"We all need someone to show us how to practice the principles we are learning."

Because we all need examples along with exhortations; demonstration along with doctrine. We all need someone to show us how to practice the principles we are learning.

God's design is that we understand the principles of His Word and then see them lived out in someone's life. This helps us put into practice these principles that God has laid out for us. Paul exhorts the Corinthian church, "Be imitators of me, just as I also am of Christ" (1 Cor. 11:1).

Remember, Paul is instructing Titus as to what to teach the women of Crete. The passage simply states: older women live godly, so that you may instruct the young women to live godly lives.

The Bible gives many illustrations that show the importance of training. Consider the pitiful pattern of Israel. Over and over again, we read of the first generation walking in obedience to God's commands, the second walking in the blessings garnered by the first, and then the third rebelling against God. The leaders failed to disciple the people, the parents failed to disciple their children, and the older men and women failed to train the younger men and women.

God expects spiritual training to occur in the home. But not every home has Christian parents, and not every Christian lives in a home that is filled with the Spirit, under the Lordship of Christ, and directed by the Word of God. So God designed the men and women in the church to train its own larger church family.

In Titus 2:3-5, God reminds older, more mature women of their responsibility to pass on what they have learned. The biblical principles of Christian living, warnings to avoid youthful mistakes and exhortations to develop Christian habits.

The main theme of Titus is about living what you believe so that others will be attracted to what you believe. God holds mature saints responsible for training the next generation to help them grow in the grace and knowledge of our Lord and Savior Jesus Christ (2 Peter 3:18). Without the principles found in Titus

"The main theme of Titus is about living what you believe so that others will be attracted to what you believe."

taught and modeled, the church is at great risk of losing the next generation.

TRAINING IS POWERFUL

The priority of spiritual training is found so often throughout both the Old and New Testaments that we cannot ignore its importance. Naomi mentored Ruth, Ezra mentored Nehemiah, Elijah mentored Elisha, Barnabus mentored Paul and Paul mentored Timothy, to name a few. The list goes on and on throughout the history of the church up to this present day.

Studies show the vast majority of what children learn from their parents is from their actions and not their words. The example of parents makes a huge difference. Of course, children need to go to church and be taught the Word of God at home, but they must also see it, hear it and watch it lived out in everyday life (Deuteronomy 6:7).

God's plan for the church is called the Great Commission. He says, "All authority has been given to Me in heaven and on earth. Go therefore and make disciples of all the nations, baptizing them in the name of the Father and the Son and the Holy Spirit, teaching them to keep all that I commanded you; and behold, I am with you always, even to the end of the age." (Matthew 28:18b-20) The main verb in this passage is "make disciples." To make a disciple involves going—that's evangelism. Baptizing—that's publicly identifying with Christ and His church.

Teaching them to obey the Word of God—that's godly living under the authority of the Lord.

Jesus left us here on this earth to train others so they would become fully committed followers of Christ. The Great Commission is a command for us to reach others and train them. He commands us to intentionally invest in relationships for the purpose of the gospel and growth in Christ for His glory. When this doesn't happen in churches like it should, there will be multitudes of people who think they're Christians, but are actually self-deceived, lost sinners. There will also be way too many immature Christians who produce only a little fruit. This is exactly what is happening today!

"Every Christian needs to be investing in others. We need to be passing the truth on to younger believers through our biblical example and biblical exhortations for God's glory."

Every Christian needs to be investing in others. We need to be passing the truth on to younger believers through our biblical example and biblical exhortations for God's glory. So we need to ask ourselves, *who will I train so they will not only continue in the faith, but also hopefully excel far beyond what I could do for the cause of Christ?* It's like a relay race. We are to pass the baton to the next runner in the race of faith.

Women who have walked with Jesus Christ for many years have much to contribute. They should pass on what they've learned. Paul is saying that mature women have the right to speak. They have lived with their husbands, they have grown along with their children, they have raised a generation, and now they must share what the Spirit has taught them. They must share both their successes and failures, passing on the principles God taught them from His Word and then forged in experience. Their lives are the basis for their instruction, and their ministry is crucial.

THE PROCESS OF TRAINING

What is the content of this training? The Bible declares that we have all we need for life and godliness within the pages of Scripture (2 Peter 1:3). Titus 2:4-5 is a fine example, because here we find a powerful curriculum for the older women to mentor the younger women: "Instruct the young women in sensibility: to love their husbands, to love their children, to be sensible, pure, workers at home, kind, being subject to their own husbands, so that the Word of God will not be slandered." These are the qualities God desires in every woman of God, whether they are single or married, going to school or working in a job—this is God's plan for godly young women.

STYLE OF TRAINING

The true biblical training described in Titus 2 is not a seminar or a sermon—it is a life-on-life personal relationship and conversation. It's a discussion about how to apply God's Word in a small group of people or even one on one. It usually means a regular time of prayer together, asking for God to work in your life over specific issues like sins you are dealing with and character qualities you are hoping to develop. It is pursuing the goals in Titus 2 with a person or persons holding you accountable to live biblically and Christlike each day.

Biblical training isn't a one-time event, a short cut to sanctification, or an instant solution. It is a long term process. It can begin with a young woman asking an older woman or a group of women to meet with her. It can begin with a godly older woman seeking out younger women to mentor. It can happen naturally, as people gather weekly in community groups. Older women can begin building relationships with younger women, intending to help them with the goals of godliness in Titus 2. This process is called discipleship—intentional relationships for the purpose of growing in Christ. Practically, it is being a friend, sharing truth, praying, holding one another accountable to follow God's Word from the heart, opening up our lives and learning from each other.

THE PURPOSES OF TRAINING

God says in Titus 2:3-4, "teaching what is good, so that they may instruct the young women in sensibility."

What exactly does it mean when God tells older women to "instruct the young women in sensibility"? He is saying that the older, more mature women have pursued godly qualities in their lives, not perfectly but progressively, and as a result have gained wisdom. They are to instruct the younger women with the wisdom God has given them as they have matured in Christ.

The words "instruct…in sensibility" are one word in the Greek text: sophronizosin. It comes from the root word sophron, which means self-controlled, prudent, thoughtful, sober, or sound. It speaks of more than dumping content; it is sharing a life in order to change a life. It is more than facts; it is communicating the attitudes of the heart.

The word sophron is used repeatedly by Paul to tell the Cretans, "Get your life in biblical order to make an impact for God's glory."

So, what does sophron training do? What are its purposes in a young woman's life? A closer look at the meaning of this Greek word yields some answers to that question.

TO HELP YOUNGER WOMEN STAY SANE IN AN INSANE WORLD

The word sophronizosin means to "make sane" or be sober-minded. The older women must help younger women to make sane judgments in a world that has gone crazy. These are just a few of the more common lies the world promotes:

- To be significant, you must have a full-time career with a big salary.
- To have an exciting life, flirt with men or cheat on your husband.
- The stereotype of husbands is being inept and wives as the stronger, wiser leader.
- Raising a godly generation of children means you are missing out on your best years.

"The job of older women is to wake up younger women so that they can see things the way they really are."

TO HELP YOUNG WOMEN PURSUE BIBLICAL PRIORITIES

Sophronizosin can also mean to restore someone to their senses. The job of older women is to wake up younger women so that they can see things the way they really are. God designed the woman's role, and apart from a closed womb or the gift of celibacy, all women are made for marriage and children. Though this seems obvious from the divine design of a woman's body, society has put incredible pressure on women to pursue a life without a husband or children.

I praise God for women who, instead of striving for the world's measure of success, fight against the current of our culture and swim upstream in support of God's plan. And all women need to help one another to do the same.

The purpose of training is to help younger women establish and maintain biblical priorities. It teaches them to value loving their husbands over finding their own identity, to love their children over having career aspirations and to live in purity over fulfilling their every desire. The purpose of training is to restore those younger in the faith to their senses so that they will begin to live according to God's priorities.

TO HELP EDUCATE YOUNGER WOMEN IN GODLINESS

A third aspect of the word sophronizosin is the reason the translation includes the word "instruct"—it means to watch, discipline, educate, encourage, advise and urge, like a school teacher does. In other words, God wants there to be a healthy relationship between older and younger women for the purpose of teaching each other toward Christlikeness through activities like praying, sharing, admonishing, correcting and counseling.

For all this to happen, the younger women must have a teachable heart. The younger are listed after the older because in God's design, they are to submit, follow and honor the older.

For mentoring to actually work in your life, you must have an attitude of submission—submission to God, to His Word and to the older Christians God has provided to lead you. If you practice submission to your parents and to the women who disciple you, then you will be better prepared to submit to your future husband and other authorities.

On the other hand, if you don't practice submission to your parents and to the women who disciple you, then you will have difficulty submitting to your husband. That's why Paul exhorts women to get this training process started as soon as possible; this training starts when you are single.

Training never works with a rebellious, independent heart. Without a teachable heart, mentoring is a waste of time. Proverbs 12:15 says, "The way of an ignorant fool is right in his own eyes, but a wise man is he who listens to counsel." If a teachable heart is present, the training process can produce great growth in both the one being mentored and in the mentor.

The only way mentoring works is for everyone involved to be in tune with Jesus Christ. Like two pianos, you can only play beautiful music together when you are both tuned with the same tuning fork—Jesus Christ. The entire Bible is filled with commands, exhortations and pleas for you to yield your life to Christ, to follow Him, trust in Him alone, cling to Him, depend upon Him, learn from Him and obey Him.

Start working on your own list of mentors and pray for God's direction. Be watching the older women in your local church and ask the Lord to show you which ones you should pursue, in order for you to grow to be more like Christ.

WHY NOT MEN?

In Titus 2 Paul says that the older women are to be training younger women, and I think it's important to note that God does not say that men should be training younger women. Though Titus was appointed by the apostle Paul to the church in Crete, Titus was not told to train the younger women. Why? Because it is not God's will that men disciple women. Men can teach women and preach God's Word to women, but not be engaged in the relational intensity of discipleship with women or the practice of training women.

The New Testament emphasizes that men minister to men and women minister to women. And there is great danger when women or men violate that New Testament norm. God designed husbands and wives to enjoy a oneness in marriage that is unique. Young husbands are to 'cleave' to their wives—literally describing a husband and wife who are welded together in every way; mentally, emotionally and physically. Outside of marriage, a strong relational bond with someone of the opposite sex can actually lead to sin. The intimate bond that God designed for marriage needs to be guarded and saved for a future spouse and not given to others prior to or outside of marriage. Just like physical intimacy was meant for marriage, the cleaving between a husband and wife was meant for marriage alone.

When a pastor counsels a woman, an unhealthy emotional bonding can be formed, potentially leading to adultery. When a young woman builds a strong friendship with an unsaved young man, that emotional intimacy may result in the woman violating Scripture and marrying an unbelieving man (1 Corinthians 7:39). That is why God's perfect design is for older women to disciple younger women and for older men to disciple younger men.

The church of Christ is paying a heavy price for violating this principle. Too many men in ministry have fallen morally because of inappropriate relationships with women. Too many born again women have married unsaved men because they did not guard their hearts from the natural process of bonding. It is so important that mature godly women counsel, disciple and train the younger women and young women seek out discipleship.

It does not have to be one special godly woman. It can be a group of older godly women. Few churches have a formal program of discipleship for women. The key is for you to pursue one or more godly women to build discipling relationships with. Become an eager learner and ask hard questions. Once trust is built, share every area of your life with them. The result of these special relationships will radically transform your life for God's glory.

FOR PERSONAL REFLECTION & GROUP DISCUSSION:

1. Do you have healthy relationships with older women? Why or why not?

2. Are you quick to seek out older godly women when you have questions or is the internet where you look for answers?

3. Are you submissive and obedient to your parents, or respectful and honoring to them if you are out of the home?

4. Who are two or three godly women you would like to begin learning from? How do you plan to ask them to disciple you?

5. List the mentors in your life and what you have learned from each of them. Identify the women who have helped you grow in Christ and those who provided worldly wisdom.

4

LET THE WOMEN BE LIKABLE & LOVING

A GODLY WOMAN LOVES HER HUSBAND

"...and in your godliness, brotherly kindness, and in your brotherly kindness, love."

2 PETER 1:7

The first thing Paul mentions to Titus when he discusses the older women training the younger women is that they should "love their husbands." This actually includes liking their husbands and by extension, being likable. The Greek word used is not the normal word for love, but one that could be translated "like."

The biblical principle is that older women train younger wives to continue liking their husbands and how to be likable. The same idea applies to single ladies toward their future husbands. Accomplishing this will take careful planning and intentional choices now. Young women should be prepared to live this way for the long term. Both singles and marrieds are well aware of how marriage can slowly decline over time. I'm sure you can identify with the reactions of this husband toward his wife's cold during the first seven years of their marriage:

The first year: "Sugar dumpling, I'm really worried about my baby girl. That's a bad sniffle, and strep is going around. I'm taking you to the hospital this afternoon for a checkup and some bedrest. I'll order food from your favorite restaurant so that you are nourished and can heal quickly.

The second year: "Listen darling, I don't like the sound of that cough. I've checked and the urgent care is open 24 hours, I'm taking you there right now."

The third year: "Maybe you'd better lie down, honey. There's nothing like a little rest when you feel lousy. I'll bring you something. Do we have any canned soup?"

The fourth year: "Now look, dear, be sensible. The kids are hungry and the sink's full of dirty dishes. After you're done fixing their meal and cleaning up the mess, maybe you should lie down and rest."

The fifth year: "Why don't you take a couple of aspirin?"

The sixth year: "I wish you would just gargle or something instead of sitting around here barking like a seal."

The seventh year: "For Pete's sake, stop sneezing! Are you trying to give me pneumonia?"

THE CHALLENGE OF LIKING AND BEING LIKABLE

Why is it that we can develop a strong love relationship and then, over time, stop liking that person? What are some difficulties that erode our enjoyment of the person to whom we have committed our lives? Whether you are evaluating your marriage, looking ahead to marriage or reflecting on a broken relationship, consider what can cause decay in a marriage.

As a pastor I've seen several life choices that tend to deteriorate the sacred bond between husbands and wives, a decline that can lead to divorce:

- Overcommitment and physical exhaustion. Young couples

who are trying to go to college, work full-time, start a family, fix up a house, volunteer at church—all at the same time.

- Excessive debt or conflict over how money is spent.
- Selfishness. When either spouse is more focused on what they are getting out of marriage, or doing what they want, rather than what they can sacrificially give toward their marriage.
- Interference from in-laws. When either the husband or wife is not fully emancipated from their parents, or if the parents won't keep a healthy distance from their married children.
- Entering into marriage with unrealistic expectations.
- Addiction to alcohol, drugs, pornography, or gambling.
- Loneliness or sexual frustration.
- Career or business failure.

"...God's design is to build a solid relationship that will last a lifetime."

These are just a few of the marriage killers that assault our relationships today, but God's design is to build a solid relationship that will last a lifetime. Remember, lasting marriages are those in which the partners have learned how to live with the unique kind of love that Paul describes to Titus. Let's take a closer look at this type of love.

The first thing God says is "to love their husbands," or it can also be translated as, to be affectionate to their husbands or to befriend their husbands. The three English words, "love their husbands," come from one Greek word, philandrous, which is used only in Titus 2:4.

Philandrous was used in classical Greek as one of the highest compliments a man could give his wife. The term was so special that it was used on many epitaphs and gravestones. One gravestone reads: "To Otacilia, my sweetest wife, who loved her husband and children and lived with me blamelessly for thirty years."

If the church is to be an effective witness to the lost, it needs to be filled with women who will diligently pursue "liking" their husbands. Again, the English text says "love," but the Greek word used emphasizes affection, appreciation and friendship.

In the New Testament there are four keys to liking your husband and becoming a likable person:

1. Understand God's **purpose** for marriage
2. Accept God's **priority** of a spouse
3. Feel God's **passion** for your spouse
4. Pursue God's **plan** to be likable

UNDERSTAND GOD'S PURPOSE FOR MARRIAGE

Let's go back to God's original design for marriage found in Genesis 1. This will help us understand what God means when He calls women to love their husbands in Titus 2:4.

God made males and females uniquely different. Genesis 1:27 says, "God created man in His own image, in the image of God He created him; male and female He created them." God made male and female for His own good purposes. In a loving, amazing, creative act, the Almighty God conceived the mysteries of male and female, masculinity and femininity to bring joy to our lives.

Just think how colorless and one-dimensional the world would be if there was only one gender! Who would want to live in an all-male or an all-female world—or for that matter, in a unisex world where all evidence of gender was ignored or suppressed? Are we not seeing this in the world today? A stamping out of the beauty of gender is causing nothing but chaos and confusion. The person who refuses to acknowledge the basic differences between male and female is blind to the beauty that God created and intended for marriage.

Marriage was designed by God to meet a problem for man: loneliness. Picture Adam, living in a perfect environment, but alone. He had fellowship with God and the company of animals. He had an interesting job too, but he was alone. God observed that this was not good. So our wise and loving Creator provided the perfect solution. He made another creature, like the man, yet wondrously unlike him. Eve was perfectly suitable for Adam–spiritually, intellectually, emotionally, and physically. According to God, she was designed to be his helper, which refers to a beneficial relationship where one person supports the other.

Marriage always begins with a need that has been there from the dawn of time, a need for companionship and completion that God understands because He Himself exists in a Trinity of three Persons who fellowship and interact with each other.

"Marriage always begins with a need that has been there from the dawn of time, a need for companionship and completion..."

Marriage was designed to bring happiness not misery. Genesis 2:23 says, "Then the man said, 'This one finally is bone of my bones, and flesh of my flesh; this one shall be called Woman, because this one was taken out of Man.'"

Here is the world's first love song! Hebrew experts tell us Adam was expressing a joyous astonishment—"At last I have someone just for me!" His phrase, "Bone of my bones and flesh of my flesh," became a favorite Old Testament saying to describe an intimate, personal relationship.

When the Lord brought the woman to Adam, the man expressed

his feelings in words similar to these: "I have finally found the one who can complete me, who takes away my loneliness, who will be as dear to me as my own flesh. She is so beautiful! She is perfectly suited to me! She is all I will ever need!"

Marriage is leaving other relationships to begin a new permanent relationship. Genesis 2:24 says, "Therefore a man shall leave his father and his mother."

Marriage begins with a leaving—leaving all other relationships. The closest relationship outside of marriage is the relationship of children to their mother and father. So if marriage requires you to leave mom and dad, then certainly all lesser relational ties must be broken, left behind or at least modified in a significant way.

Practically speaking, leaving means that housekeeping, women's Bible studies, social media, career and volunteer work should not take priority over the relationship a wife enjoys with her husband. Leaving also means that the man must be willing to limit activities like gaming, sports, TV, ministry, and career in order to develop the strongest relationship with his wife.

Marriage requires an inseparable joining of a husband and wife until death. Genesis 2:24 adds, "Therefore a man shall leave his father and his mother, and cleave to his wife; and they shall become one flesh."

What does "be joined" mean (or "cleaving" in the old English)? It means an unwavering loyalty, a spiritual gluing, a continual love that will not let go no matter what. A wife and husband commit to never say or do anything that would drive a wedge between them. You can love someone you respect and you can love someone you trust. Commitment in marriage means avoiding anything that would undermine trust and respect.

Marriage means oneness in the fullest sense, including intimate physical union without shame. Genesis 2:24 concludes, "Therefore a man shall leave his father and his mother, and shall cleave to his wife; and they shall become one flesh." Then verse 25 adds, "And the man and his wife were both naked and were not ashamed."

In the divine pattern for marriage, sexual intercourse between husband and wife includes both an intimate physical knowledge and an intimate personal knowledge of each other. So leaving, cleaving and knowing each other results in a new identity in which two individuals merge into one—they become one in mind, heart, body and spirit. That is why divorce is so devastating.

But if marriage is so great, why does God have to exhort young women to love their husbands in Titus 2? Why do godly older women need to train younger women to love their husbands? Doesn't it come naturally for them to practice God's pattern for marriage?

The answer is no. Most of the marriages on Crete in the first century were arranged by the families for political, financial or other purposes. Marriage did not exist on the basis of love or romance in that culture. So at that time it was crucial for women to learn to love their husbands. And in today's cultural climate of sexual promiscuity, feminism, machismo, spousal abuse and a high divorce rate, we have just as much need for God to call us to like our spouses and become likable in our relationships. So, what else can we learn about how to do that?

"...it is important to be reading and meditating on Scripture, so that our minds can be renewed by God's truth, particularly about marriage."

In today's culture, we try to pursue marriage based on love and romance. However, because the mainstream media promotes sexual freedom, feminism and machismo, our idea of love and romance can be defined by the world instead of Scripture. That's why it is important to be reading and meditating on Scripture, so that our minds can be renewed by God's truth, particularly about marriage.

ACCEPT GOD'S PRIORITY OF A SPOUSE

When God says that young women are to love their husbands, He knows that...

- You have His grace working in your heart
- You are filled and empowered by the Spirit
- You are motivated by the example of Christ
- You want to obey His Word from your heart
- You desire to be an effective witness for Christ
- You have His glory as your highest goal

"Loving her husband is listed first in the essential qualities, and it must be first in the heart, mind, and priorities of a wife."

In other words, these qualities assume that you have a genuine relationship with Jesus Christ.

Then the very first duty of the Christian woman, after following Jesus Christ, is to love her husband. Loving her husband is listed first in the essential qualities, and it must be first in the heart, mind, and priorities of a wife. God is highlighting two key truths when He mentions loving husbands first in this list of essential qualities.

First, loving your spouse is a mutual responsibility. God tells women, "Love your husbands." You have just as much responsibility to love him as he does to love you. When both wife and husband serve each other as an expression of their love, their affection and appreciation will blossom too.

" No one can say they love the Lord without liking the Lord relationally."

Second, loving your spouse is essential. Most passages describing a Christian's love for God and their love for other believers use the Greek word agape. Agape is the type of love that is sacrificial service. Yet in using agape to describe our relationships with the Lord and each other, the author is not negating phileo love: the liking, caring, and enjoying friendship-type love. No one can say they love the Lord without liking the Lord relationally. You can't really love another Christian without also liking them to some degree. When you demonstrate agape love, there must be some level of phileo love too.

When you read 1 John 4:20, you not only hear sacrificial agape love, but relationship phileo love is also implied. "If someone says, 'I love God,' and hates his brother [or spouse], he is a liar; for the one who does not love his brother [or spouse] whom he has seen, cannot love God whom he has not seen." In Matthew 5:23-24 Jesus reminds you to maintain a right relationship with others, or you will not be right with God. "If you are presenting your offering at the altar, and there remember that your brother [or spouse] has something against you, leave your offering there before the altar and go; first be reconciled to your brother [or spouse], and then come and present your offering." Loving the Lord means you will have a right relationship with your husband which includes both liking and loving him.

Paul tells Titus that teaching women to like their husbands

is first on God's list. No career, school, ministry, child, parent, boss or goal should ever stand in the way of the love relationship between a wife and husband. More specifically, nothing should ever hinder a wife from fulfilling her duty to like her husband.

Here are four questions to ask yourself if you are seeking to build biblical habits that will serve your marriage for a lifetime.

1. Does your husband get your best or the leftovers?
2. Do you make things special for your husband or are your actions towards him routine, while everyone else (children, friends, parents, church) gets the special treatment?
3. Do you work hard at trying to please him?
4. Does your husband work harder in the marriage than you do?

"Remember, loving your husband is an expression of loving the Lord."

You will never grow to love your husband the way God wants you to unless you first accept that loving your spouse should be your top priority next to loving the Lord. Remember, loving your husband is an expression of loving the Lord.

FEEL GOD'S PASSION FOR YOUR SPOUSE

The godly woman also recognizes that her love is more than mere obedience. The Greek verb in "love your husbands" is not agape, the totally unselfish love that has the capacity to keep on giving without expecting anything in return. Rather, it uses the Greek verb phileo as its root and speaks of a love that cherishes with tender affection. It is the love of relationship, sharing, communication and friendship. You are to not only to love your husband, but you are also to like him.

Why do so many Christians miss this responsibility and blessing? Because you and I can easily drift from an internally motivated love to an external, empty, routine or self-centered love. We can let our schedule drive our obedience rather than our heart commitment. This can also happen between us and God. We let the daily routine run our lives and forget that Christianity is a love relationship.

Many Christians have the outward appearance of being obedient to God and do all that's required of them without remaining tenderhearted toward Christ. Those who do this may appear spiritual, but if they continue with only an external faith, they've lost their first love (Revelation 2:4).

A marriage relationship can also drift into that same kind of sad mediocrity, eroding from love to mere duty. You do what is required with an outward obedience, but inwardly your heart is no longer tender and affectionate toward your spouse. You may even sink to a level where you no longer like him. You must learn how to continue to appreciate him as a best friend, a lover, a provider, a leader—as someone you continually cherish.

Let me suggest some possible indicators of whether you like your husband—answer these questions yes or no. (Single women can pray and plan for the future as you read them.)

- Do you greet him at the door? Do your eyes light up when you see him?
- Do you laugh at his jokes, even when they are not that funny?
- Do you cheer him on when he is in a competition?
- Do you hold his hand, show affection, give gifts and surprise him unexpectedly?
- Do you make time to communicate and connect heart to heart?

The answers to these questions can identify whether a woman likes her husband. Developing this kind of love will require some mentoring from a godly older woman and dependence upon the

Holy Spirit. God can sanctify your heart to love in this way.

Some of you married women may be thinking, I could never love my husband that way! He's a crude beast, shoving food in his mouth, burping, pawing at me and changing channels like he's possessed. But God says in 2 Peter 1:3, "His divine power has granted to us everything pertaining to life and godliness, through the full knowledge of Him who called us by His own glory and excellence." God can change your heart to love him and apply grace and forgiveness.

"God can change your heart to love him and apply grace and forgiveness."

Sometimes wives harbor a list of wrongs done by their husbands. When thoughts of affection arise so does the competing record of your husband's offenses. Seek to deal with each item on your list so that you are able to confess your sin and put to death the root of bitterness that has sprung up and caused trouble in your marriage (Hebrews 12:15). Remember 1 Corinthians 13:5 tells us to keep no record of wrongs.

PURSUE GOD'S PLAN TO BE LIKABLE

Here is a key to growing in love with your spouse, and also to finding a spouse. As you seek to become a more likable person, you will make it easier for him to like you and vice versa. Young single women, if you make this a goal, you will be more attractive to a man who is seeking a godly wife.

So, how can you be more likable, according to the Scriptures? Here are five qualities to develop and demonstrate:

A PASSIONATE DESIRE TO BE LIKE JESUS

The heart of the matter is the matter of the heart. Unless you have a passionate desire to be like Jesus, no amount of outward works will make you a godly woman. But what you do outwardly does demonstrate what is in your heart. If you want to know whether you are passionately desiring to be like Christ, here are a few practical tests.

Check your reputation. You can fool some of the people some of the time, but you can't fool all of the people all of the time. 1 Timothy 5:10 says that widows are to have "a reputation for good works." Proverbs 22:1 says that, "A good name is to be chosen over great wealth," and Ecclesiastes 7:1 says "better is a good name than good oil [riches]."

When her godliness is authentic, a woman will have a good reputation. People will notice and talk about how she loves the Lord and puts Jesus first in both her private and public life. Eventually, what someone is in private becomes known in public.

Check your appearance. The way you dress tells you something about your heart. This is implied by Paul's words in 1 Timothy 2:9-10, "I want women to adorn themselves with proper clothing, with modesty and self-restraint, not with braided hair and gold or pearls or costly clothing, but rather by means of good works, as is proper for women professing godliness."

God is not telling women to dress dumpy or dull, but a godly woman will dress modestly (literally, "without any shame"), reflecting a heart that desires to point to God. Here are some things she considers:

- What is exposed, because that is what draws the attention of people.
- How tight her clothes fit, because it draws more attention to those physical features.

When I was a junior high pastor, the staff women used to plan a "girls-only time" to show the 7th, 8th, and 9th grade girls what they look like when they dress immodestly. In a private room, the staff girls would act out everyday activities while wearing some of the current clothing trends, and the girls would scream with laughter over how inappropriate they looked. But the point was made clearly without setting up external legalistic rules. Young women need to understand the difference between attractive and alluring.

Modesty is not just about clothing. A common theme on social media today is posting a picture or video of yourself with a sultry look, fluttering eyes or provocative posture while writing a verse below the picture. When people look at your social media presence, do they see a page that points to you or a page that points to Christ?

Parents should lovingly tell their daughters what guys think as they look at a woman dressed immodestly. Sadly, this does not happen very often today. But it is crucial that women understand the male propensity to leer and lust, especially when clothing is not modest. The woman who really loves the Lord will dress with the motive of trying to honor Christ with her appearance.

"The woman who really loves the Lord will dress with the motive of trying to honor Christ with her appearance."

Check your focus. A godly woman may have many responsibilities but will have a singular focus. Only one thing is really important to her: "Whether, then, you eat or drink or whatever you do, do all to the glory of God" (1 Corinthians 10:31).

In the midst of all they do, godly women will want to bring glory to God, to point to Him, to make Him look good. This priority will show through when they talk, work, play, drive, watch entertainment, surf the internet and live everyday life.

A godly woman will have a passionate desire to be like Jesus. And this desire will show itself in various areas of her life. So, how does this make her likable? When you desire to be like Jesus and show it in your actions, your life becomes a sweet aroma. In 2 Corinthians 2:14-15 it says, "Thanks be to God, who always leads us in triumphal procession in Christ, and manifests through us the aroma of the knowledge of Him in every place. For we are a fragrance of Christ to God among those who are being saved and among those who are perishing."

Don't you just love the smell of cinnamon rolls in your house, or your favorite scented candle? When you live with a passionate desire to be like Jesus, you will be a sweet aroma to others. Genuine born again believers are not crusty, they are cheerful; they are not depressing but delightful to be around.

A DISCIPLINED AND DEPENDENT LIFESTYLE

A godly woman understands she can't live the Christian life on her own—Jesus must live the Christian life through her. She grows disciplined in her walk with Christ as she daily depends upon the power of the Spirit. This is the only way she is able to love and like her husband and become more likable in his eyes.

She has learned the discipline of practicing Galatians 5:16. She seeks to walk by the Spirit and refrain from carrying out the desire of the flesh. An empowered walk comes from learning the disciplines of moment-by-moment dependence upon the Holy Spirit, by keeping your eyes focused on Jesus, learning to pray without ceasing and meditating on the Word of God. She will seek after Him every moment of every day, confessing her sin and yielding her life to Him.

How does this make you likable? Simple—when you develop the disciplines of a Christ-like lifestyle and seek each day to be filled with the Spirit, then your personality, words, attitudes and actions will produce a special kind of fruit: the fruit of the Spirit.

Which kind of fruit do you produce? Is it "sexual immorality, impurity, sensuality, idolatry, sorcery, enmities, strife, jealousy, outbursts of anger, selfish ambition, dissensions, factions, envying, drunkenness, carousing" (Galatians 5:19-21, the works of the flesh)? Or is it "love, joy, peace, patience, kindness, goodness, faithfulness, gentleness, self-control" (Galatians 5:22-23, the fruit of the Spirit)?

Who would not want to be around someone who is loving, joyful, peaceful, patient, kind, good, faithful, gentle, and self-controlled? Of course a husband would like those qualities in his wife.

"Demanding our rights is the way of our society, but giving up our rights is the way of God."

A HUMBLE SUBMISSION TO AUTHORITY

Demanding our rights is the way of our society, but giving up our rights is the way of God. The Bible says, "There is no authority except from God, and those which exist have been appointed by God" (Romans 13:1).

Since God appoints all the authorities in our lives, He is calling us to submit to His authority by honoring those He has placed in authority. The only exception is when an authority tries to force us to sin or disobey the Scripture in some manner. Citizens are to submit to and honor their government (Romans 13:1-2). Children are to submit to and honor their parents (Ephesians 6:1). Congregations are to submit to and honor their eldership (Hebrews 13:17). Employees are to submit to and honor their employers (Colossians 3:22). Wives are to submit to and honor their husbands.

> *Wives, be subject to your own husbands, as to the Lord...the wife must see to it that she respects her husband. (Ephesians 5:22, 33)*

> *In the same way, you wives, be subject to your own husbands so that even if any of them are disobedient to the word, they may be won without a word by the conduct of their wives, as they observe your pure conduct with fear...For in this way in former times the holy women also, who hoped in God, used to adorn themselves, being subject to their own husbands, just as Sarah obeyed Abraham, calling him lord. You have become her children if you do good, not fearing any intimidation. (1 Peter 3:1-6)*

Someone who is truly submissive will not create strife or contention. Consider these warnings from Proverbs. "It is better to live in a corner of a roof, than in a house shared with a contentious woman" (21:9). "It is better to live in a desert land, than with a contentious [strife-filled] and vexing [angry] woman" (21:19). "A constant dripping on a day of steady rain and a contentious woman are alike" (27:15).

God is obviously saying that an angry, strife-filled, non-submissive, rebellious woman is not likable. But God calls a submissive wife a treasure: "An excellent wife, who can find? For her worth is far above pearls" (Proverbs 31:10).

"A godly woman is likable because she has a heart to meet needs and help others.

A HEART TO PLEASE AND SERVE

A godly woman is likable because she has a heart to meet needs and help others. Proverbs 31:20 says, "She extends her hand to the poor, and she stretches out her hands to the needy." And Proverbs 31:27 says, "She watches over the ways of her household, and does not eat the bread of idleness."

A godly wife demonstrates a heart willing to meet her husband's needs, even in the area of physical intimacy:

> *But because of sexual immoralities, each man is to have his own wife, and each woman is to have her own husband. The husband must fulfill his duty to his wife, and likewise also the wife to her husband. The wife does not have authority over her own body, but the husband does; and likewise also the husband does not have authority over his own body, but the wife does. Stop depriving one another, except by agreement for a time, so that you may devote yourselves to prayer, and come together again so that Satan will not tempt you because of your lack of self-control. (1 Corinthians 7:2-5)*

This passage contains four commands from God directed at spouses to take care of each other physically in marriage. A godly wife does not withhold herself from her husband, she understands that physical intimacy with her husband is as holy as any other

"All godly people, male and female, feel concern about the next generation being saved..."

act she renders unto the Lord, such as Bible reading and prayer. And, in that way and many others, she not only loves him but is a likable partner.

A DESIRE TO DISCIPLE

A godly woman not only wants to bear children, but she longs to disciple and train them to follow Christ. This is why the next godly quality Paul lists in Titus 2 for young women to develop is to love their children.

All godly people, male and female, feel concern about the next generation being saved, sanctified, made spiritually strong and morally pure—not only their own children, but the next generation in the church. This kind of concern makes a person likable. They also want to share what God has taught them, to help others live lives that are pleasing to Christ and encourage those weak in the faith.

Are you likable? Do you have a passion to be like Christ, to live in dependence upon Christ's power, to submit to God-appointed authority with a heart seeking to please, and to mentor others toward godliness? All the truths discussed in this chapter are equally beneficial to both single and married women. Single women who make godliness their highest goal are more likely to attract godly men. A Christian marriage built on a relationship between two people like this will produce incredible joy for both—and together they will be a fantastic witness for Christ.

Remember, only Christ can transform you to live this way. Religious activities can change your habits, but only a relationship with Jesus can change your heart. Turn to Christ now and depend upon Him alone.

FOR PERSONAL REFLECTION & GROUP DISCUSSION:

1. Have you or has anyone you know faced any of the marital challenges mentioned early in this chapter and overcome them? How did that happen?

2. Why do you think God tells young women to love their husbands before He tells them to love their children?

3. Do you think you are a likable person? Why or why not?

4. What kind of reputation do you have? What would those closest to you say?

5. Set one goal this week for how you can better like and love your husband. If you are not married, then determine one way you can improve liking and loving your parents or siblings.

5

LET THE WOMEN BE TRAINING & NURTURING

A GODLY WOMAN LOVES CHILDREN

"But she will be saved through the bearing of children, if they continue in faith and love and sanctification with self-restraint."

1 TIMOTHY 2:15

Husbands commonly ask their wives about their day when they return home from work. Here is an example:

"So, what did you do today?" Ramona's husband asked. Ramona stood up, brandishing a dangerously held fork. "What did I do today?" she asked. Walking toward him, still holding the fork, she repeats, "What did I do today?" She hands him a piece of paper.

What I Did Today

3:21 am	Woke up. Took Jeffrey to bathroom.
3:31 am	Woke up. Took Jeffrey to bed.
3:46 am	Got you to quit snoring.
3:49 am	Went to sleep.
5:11 am	Woke up. Took Jeffrey to bathroom.

6:50 am	Alarm went off. Mentally reviewed all I had to do today. Hit snooze button.
7:00 am	Alarm went off. Hit snooze button.
7:10 am	Alarm went off. Contemplated doing something violent to alarm clock.
7:19 am	Got up. Got dressed. Warned Stephen.
7:21 am	Made bed. Warned Stephen.
7:25 am	Spanked Stephen. Helped Stephen. Prayed with Stephen.
7:37 am	Fed boys a breakfast consisting of Cheerios, orange juice, and something that resembled toast. Scolded Jeffrey for mixing them all together.
7:46 am	Woke Rachael.
7:48 am	Had devotions (2 minutes).
7:50 am	Made Stephen's lunch. Tried to answer Jeffrey's question, "Why does God need people?" Warned Stephen.
8:01 am	Woke Rachael.
8:02 am	Started laundry.
8:03 am	Took rocks out of the washing machine.
8:04 am	Started laundry.
8:13 am	Planned grocery list. Tried to answer Jeffrey's question, "Why do we need God?"
8:29 am	Woke Rachael.
8:30 am	Helped Stephen with homework. Told
8:31 am	him to remember his lunch. Sent Stephen to school.
8:32 am	Had breakfast with Rachael—oatmeal. Pulled toast out of game console. Warned Jeffrey. Rest of morning—Teacher phoned wondering why Stephen had no socks. Took them to him. Returned

	library books. Explained why a cover was missing. Mailed letters. Bought groceries. Shut Netflix off. Scrolled through Facebook. Texted Sherri and Julie about prayer requests. Cleaned house. Wiped noses. Wiped windows. Wiped bottoms. Teacher called wondering why Stephen had no lunch. Took it to him. Pulled spaghetti out of carpet.
12:35 pm	Put wet clothes in dryer.
12:36 pm	Sat down to rest.
12:39 pm	Scolded Jeffrey. Helped him put clothes back in dryer.
12:45 pm	Agreed to babysit for a friend. Cut tree sap out of Rachael's hair.
	Early afternoon—Regretted babysitting decision. Killed assorted insects. Read to the kids. Clipped ten fingernails. Sent kids outside. Unpacked groceries. Watered plants. Swept floor. Explained to Jeffrey why he shouldn't fry ants with a magnifying glass.
	Late afternoon—Put Band-Aids on knees. Organized task force to clean kitchen. Accepted appointment to local committee (secretary said, "We thought you would have extra time since you don't work"). Tried to answer Rachael's question, "Why are boys and girls different?" Listened to a zillion more questions. Answered a few. Briefly considered making dinner. Briefly considered heading for the hills.
5:21 pm	Husband came home looking for food, quietness, and romance.

"Of course, not all my days go this smoothly." Then she asked him while still brandishing the fork—"Any questions?"

It is no wonder that, in the Bible, God reminds women that they should love and like their children. Titus 2:4 says that the older women should "instruct the young women…to love their children." To outsiders looking at motherhood, loving children might seem like an easy thing to do. *How can anyone not like kids?* they might think, *nothing is more entertaining than being around kids and watching them grow up.*

Here's an example of why people think that:

A six-year-old boy has been telling his first grade teacher for weeks about the baby brother or sister that was expected at his house. Then one day the mother allowed the boy to feel the movements of the unborn child in her belly. The six-year-old was obviously impressed but made no comment. But after that day, he stopped telling his teacher about the impending event. So the teacher, curious about the change in the boy, finally asked him, "Tommy, whatever became of that baby brother or sister you were expecting at home?" Tommy burst into tears and confessed, "I think Mommy ate it!"

You can't help but love kids for the things they come up with, right? Yet, for certain people, there are few things more difficult than loving their children.

When all three kids in a family wake up in a bad mood, whine and scream for things they don't really want, refuse to eat any meal without severe complaint, find a box of cookies and eat a

"Loving children is more than just a matter of natural instincts—it is a spiritual ministry…"

dozen each, play with the buttons on the computer, throw a ball through the living room window, torture the dog next door, eat the house plants and write on the wall with permanent markers—after all that, a mother may not be feeling a great deal of love for her children. The same could be said for single women who care for children as a job, ministry volunteer, or family member.

WHY WOMEN SHOULD LOVE CHILDREN

Loving children is more than just a matter of natural instincts—it is a spiritual ministry that is near to the heart of God and utterly indispensable to His Kingdom plan. Yet this priority has been lost to most women in our current culture.

THE SPIRITUAL WAR AGAINST CHILDREN

Paul tells Titus that the older women should mentor the younger women to love their children because on Crete there were a lot of bad attitudes and practices to be overcome. Raising kids in the first century was a duty the woman inherited with the marriage her parents arranged for her. However, children were also considered a burden since they meant more mouths to feed. Typically, in Greek and Roman society, people were so lacking in natural affection that the weak, deformed and sometimes female infants were abandoned and left to die. This was an accepted pattern of life.

It's not much different in our culture today, whereby the best estimates I've seen, an abortion occurrs about every 30 seconds in the U.S. And, more than ten kids run away from home every hour. Abusive beatings and psychological trauma have become common occurrences. Our hearts scream at the terrible injustices against children.

I think you can evaluate any culture by its treatment of two groups of people—senior citizens and children. We could talk about how Christians often mirror the unsaved world's worship

"I think you can evaluate any culture by its treatment of two groups of people—senior citizens and children."

of youth and denigration of the aged. Think about just children specifically—most young American couples are more interested in finding a nice place to live than investing in children. This is a warped priority. Countries like Canada are encouraging a "one child" family campaign with slogans like, "The most loving thing you can give your first child is not to have another."

This disease in our culture has infected the church as well. More and more Christian women are viewing motherhood as a burden to perform, rather than a gift from the Lord. The world keeps telling women that the role of the mother is second best, and as a nation we have bought that lie. According to a recent U.S. Census, more than 40% of the children in the U.S. are being dropped off at daycare centers or locked indoors as latchkey kids so that mom can pursue a career. Yet according to God's Word, being a full-time mother is one of the highest privileges and greatest influences a woman can have.

THE SPIRITUAL IMPORTANCE OF MOTHERHOOD

1 Timothy 2:15 makes a very dramatic statement about the importance of motherhood. Paul says that through raising godly children, women—as a category of people—can be relieved of the stigma of producing a cursed race of people: "But she will be saved through the bearing of children, if they continue in faith and love and sanctification with self-restraint."

What does that mean? It doesn't mean women must have children to be saved, but it does mean even though the sin of one woman (Eve) resulted in generations of cursed children, now the righteousness of one woman (a mother who's in Christ) can produce generations of godly children.

That is the point. Women are delivered from the stigma of the fall when a mother's investment in the lives of her children results in them continuing in faith, love and self-control. Simply, if a woman maintains her godliness, her trust in God's Word, a genuine love for God and purity of life, there will be an increased possibility that she will raise children who will be a blessing to the church and the world, rather than a curse.

If, by God's grace, a godly woman can raise a generation of godly children, this will lead exponentially to many more believers in Christ. So never forget that God has chosen to use the ministry of mothers in a special way to draw their children to Himself. Never minimize the power of a mother's influence.

What does the big, burly football player say when the camera is turned on him? "Hi..." (Hi, who?) "Hi, Mom." Why? Because it was mom who shaped and impacted his life more than anyone else.

THE SPIRITUAL NEEDS OF CHILDREN

Another reason why women should love children is that children have one basic problem: they lack wisdom. Even sinless Jesus, when he was a child, needed to grow in various ways. Luke 2:52 says he "was advancing in wisdom and stature, and in favor with God and men." That verse outlines four areas in which children need to grow: wisdom (mental needs), stature (physical needs), favor with man (social needs) and favor with God (spiritual needs). If the sinless Savior could grow in those areas, imagine how much sinful children lack and need to grow in them!

Children lack **wisdom**. They lack instruction and knowledge. They lack the ability to apply the truth of God's Word to everyday life. When babies come into the world, their brains are sponges for soaking up information. They are born with an evil bent, but without knowledge and how to live by truth. What they are going to know must first be taught to them then modeled for them.

Children also lack **discretion**. They don't know what's right and wrong. They don't recognize danger. They don't know not to chew on extension cords or poke things into electrical outlets. These things must be taught.

Children lack **stature**. They are weak physically and unable to support or sustain themselves. Parents are responsible for feeding them, nourishing them, and making sure they get the proper rest. Parents must protect them, direct them, schedule for them, dress them and so much more. Children can't fend for themselves; they can't make it in the world alone.

Children lack proper **social** behavior. They are unable to get along with others because social training takes time. The dominant trait of a toddler is selfishness. He can't conceive of anything beyond "I want it now" and "It's mine." It's difficult to teach children to share. They don't know the social graces of humility and unselfishness. These things must be taught, trained, modeled, and encouraged.

Children lack **favor** with God. As the result of the fall, children are born into sin. Spiritually, they do not come into the world with a natural love for God. When they are little, they may comprehend God to some degree. But without proper instruction and modeling, children will drift away from the knowledge of the Lord. Ephesians 6:4 says, "Do not provoke your children to anger, but bring them up in the discipline and instruction of the Lord." This is the responsibility of parents.

"As parents, you are responsible for providing an environment that helps your children mature..."

Children will encounter problems in all four dimensions of life—mental, physical, social, and spiritual. As parents, you are responsible for providing an environment that helps your children mature in these areas of inadequacy. If you fail to provide for their growth, you will produce "a generation that curses its father and does not bless its mother…a generation that is clean in its own eyes, yet is not washed from its filthiness" (Proverbs 30:11-12).

Why does God tell mothers to love their children? Because it should be their priority in life and ministry to meet the spiritual needs of the next generation of God's people. And no one can do that better than a mother.

HOW WOMEN CAN LOVE CHILDREN

What does it mean for a woman to love her children, or for a single woman to prepare for motherhood? For some moms, loving children gets harder the older the children become. Take this conversation between a mom and her twenty-something son:

> Mom: Why don't you get yourself a job?
> Son: Why?
> Mom: So you can earn some money.
> Son: Why?
> Mom: So you could put some money in a bank account and earn interest.
> Son: Why?
> Mom: So when you're old you can use the money in your bank account, and you'll never have to work again.
> Son: But I'm not working now!

It can be tough to direct children biblically, but God exhorts women to love their children, even adult children. Never give up on them. Accept them, minister to them, sacrifice for them and most importantly, learn to really like them, cherish them, and delight in them.

For the single woman, this means that you should be around kids now; become the favorite sitter or "auntie" to a family. Learn the ins and outs of caring for kids. Watch a godly couple raise their children. Having godly older mothers in your life will prepare you to love your own children someday. Many single women have had very little instruction or modeling on motherhood and taking steps now is crucial to prepare for the future.

The Greek word for "love their children" in Titus 2:4 is much like the word used for "love their husbands" in the same verse, which includes liking them. This means to love children in ways that affectionately care—appreciating, cherishing, enjoying and liking them.

THE PREREQUISITES FOR LOVING CHILDREN

What kind of a woman can commit to this kind of love? How can she like children when they drive her crazy, break her heart, drain her dry and disturb her sleep? How can a mom avoid the pitfall of focusing on their child's happiness instead of their Christlikeness? By studying the pattern given us in the New Testament epistles, we learn this:

You must first be transformed by Christ. Only by knowing Christ personally can you live for others and not only for yourself. Jesus said, "Come to Me, all who are weary and heavy-laden, and I will give you rest" (Matthew 11:28) and "I came that they may have life, and have it abundantly" (John 10:10). And 2 Corinthians 5:15 says, "He died for all, so that they who live would no longer live for themselves, but for Him who died and rose again on their behalf." No woman can live like Christ without Christ living in her.

You must be fully functioning in the church. When Paul tells mothers to love their children in Titus 2, he is not talking to women who had an independent, self-defined, solo-saint

Christianity. That kind of Christianity didn't exist on Crete as it does in our culture. Paul was addressing young women who were functioning in a community of Christians. They were involved in ministry, living under the authority of godly elders, receiving instruction regularly from the Word of God and being mentored by older women.

Women who do not regularly attend church, serve in ministry, participate in a small group, regularly study the Word and pray with fellow believers are not going to raise godly children. The godly mom realizes she does not have all the spiritual gifts and needs the church to help train her children to be Christlike.

"You and your children will only understand Christ fully in the context of an assembly of Christians."

You and your children will only understand Christ fully in the context of an assembly of Christians. It is one of the reasons why the New Testament calls the church the body of Christ—a physical manifestation of Christ on the earth. When all the parts of the body function the way God designed, everyone sees more of Christ and becomes more like Christ (Ephesians 4:16).

You must be depending upon the Holy Spirit. The two New Testament passages directed most clearly and specifically at parents, Ephesians 6:4 and Colossians 3:21, are preceded by commands to be under the control of the Holy Spirit and saturated in the Word of God. That means a godly woman daily confesses her sins, denies her desires, follows the truth of Scripture and depends on the Holy Spirit to empower her to be a mother. Biblical mothering requires the supernatural power of God through you!

When the godly mother yields to the Holy Spirit in obedience to the Word of God, she will experience the fruit of the Spirit. And love is the first fruit listed in Galatians 5! This is how a mom is able to love her children even when their behavior is truly unlovable.

You must be following Christ's plan. In order to love your children, you must totally reject the world's ideas about women and motherhood. You must reject the pictures of women being painted by the media—the princess warrior, the wimpy doormat, the bathing suit seductress, the sarcastic comic comeback artist, the picture-perfect influencer and the frontier feminist.

What is Christ's plan? It's right there in Titus 2. The only way for a woman to love her children the way her Creator designed is to come to Christ, function in the church community, be filled with God's Spirit daily and follow God's plan provided in Titus 2.

THE PRACTICE OF LOVING CHILDREN

Let's more closely examine how a woman loves her children according to the biblical pattern. Also, what steps must a single woman take in order to be prepared to be a godly mom? Again, you don't become a Christlike wife the day you get married and you don't become a godly mom the day you give birth. These are qualities that must be pursued and developed before you get married and have kids and they will continue to develop through the years.

Chapter six of Deuteronomy provides a historical backdrop for Titus 2. After forty years of wandering in the desert, the Israelites were finally ready to enter the Promised Land. Moses calls the Israelites to prepare themselves for this momentous event. High on the priority list was his instruction to invest in their families—because the family is high on God's priority list. There were no synagogues at this time, and the burden to educate and train children fell completely upon their families. So we can learn from this passage at least three practical ways that a mom can love her children.

Model obedience to God's Word. In Deuteronomy 6:4-6,

Moses says a strong family must have hearts committed to God's truth: "Hear, O Israel! Yahweh is our God, Yahweh is one! You shall love Yahweh your God with all your heart and with all your soul and with all your might. These words, which I am commanding you today, shall be on your heart."

First, God's Word was written to be obeyed. God isn't mumbling or giving opinions when He speaks. The very moment He speaks, we are obligated to respond. Our intellect, emotions, body and will should all be captivated by the truth of God's Word. Our response should be the total commitment of our entire being—heart, soul, mind and strength.

If you intend to raise your children to live for God, this is the issue that must be settled right from the start. Does your life reflect that the Word of God is your authority? If you are going to see your children follow the Lord, you must follow His Word. And your children must see that you follow God's Word as the most important and trustworthy guide for all of life.

As I shepherd my church and talk to parents, I can often determine whether God's Word is their authority or not by asking some key questions like these: Are both Dad and Mom involved in the discipleship and discipline of the children? Are biblical principles the foundation of the home?

Second, God's Word must be on your hearts because as His children you will want to please your Father. In Deuteronomy 6:6, when God says through Moses that His commands should be "on your heart," that phrase means to bear a heavy weight or concern. It refers to something you think about and pay attention to.

Christian parents often fail to impact their children spiritually because their own hearts have grown cold to God's truth. How does that happen? Often it's the result of allowing their relationship with the Lord to become routine.

I used to pray, "Lord, change my children," and nothing happened. Then one day it dawned on me, and I began to pray, "Lord, change me." To the extent that you allow God to change

"To the extent that you allow God to change your life, He will equip you to become a better discipler because your actions will back up His Word."

your life, He will equip you to become a better discipler because your actions will back up His Word.

Make your home a biblical training environment. Deuteronomy 6:7 says, "You shall teach them diligently to your sons and shall speak of them when you sit in your house and when you walk by the way and when you lie down and when you rise up." Circle the two verbs—"speak" and "teach." These are the primary means by which you will disciple your children and the tools God has given you to train them.

"Teach" is the formal word for instruction. In the Hebrew it literally means to point in a direction. You are showing your kids which way to go. The New Testament specifically says that Dad is to teach. If there is no dad in the home, then Mom is to teach. The church is not a substitute for parents, but a complement to help parents teach. Student ministry provides younger models for young students, but is not a substitute for the instruction and modeling of parents. There needs to be structured learning in the home.

Notice Moses says, back in verse 7, "teach them diligently." The Hebrew word for "diligently" means to sharpen through repetition, as in sharpening a sword. It's not a product of luck, but of continual effort. Investing in your family doesn't happen by accident. So, how does this kind of commitment work? One way is to set a goal of having a family table time—one, two, three or more times a week.

Here's a helpful guide for how young mothers can practice the idea of a family time at the table:

T-A-B-L-E

Tune: sing fun songs, hymns, choruses, play instruments
Ask/Adore: make prayer personal and add praise and thanksgiving. Use pictures to pray.
Bible: read it, act it out, be creative
Love: plan a ministry together—to seniors, needy kids or a neighborhood outreach
Enjoy: laugh a lot, include treats—make it fun so they look forward to it each time

In Deuteronomy 6:7, Moses not only says to teach God's commands to your children, but he also says you should "speak of them" in all circumstances of life. This is referring to informal instruction, which involves spontaneous learning—a valuable, effective and fruitful way to learn. While having regular family devotions is important, unexpected opportunities for training up your children are incredible gifts from God. It is also important for parents to view events in daily life as opportunities for informal instruction. Recognize these opportunities when you are shopping, house cleaning, participating in sports, meal prep and even family vacations.

The "talking" in Deuteronomy 6:7 does not happen in a classroom. So, when do you do it? Moses says, "When you sit in your house." That presupposes that you sit in your house. Many homes are like an airport terminal where people are moving in all different directions. Parents and children are often crossing paths without much interaction. ("Hi, who are you?"—"I'm your mother."—"Really?")

When was the last time you walked with your child and kept your mouth shut? By just being together you're communicating powerful messages—more powerful than you'll ever understand. We make very little time to build relationships, do things together and have fun. Discipling your children takes time. It must be both quantity and quality time.

"We make very little time to build relationships, do things together, and have fun. Discipling your children takes time. It must be both quantity and quality time."

When Moses says "when you lie down and when you rise up," he is using a Hebrew expression that includes the totality of life—everything that occurs in between morning and night. But you won't talk about the Lord the first thing in the morning and the last thing at night and everywhere in between unless He is on your heart. Whatever is on your heart is what you'll talk about the most.

I suggest that you turn shopping trips, home projects, sports, games and other events into practical biblical learning lessons. Make vacations not only times for fun memories but also opportunities to talk of the Lord in natural conversations. Talk about Him in everything from camping to hiking, the beauty of His creation and the blessings of family.

In the Scriptures, God gives parents another tool to aid in their instruction of children: loving, controlled, wisely applied discipline. Proverbs 22:15 says, "Folly is bound up in the heart of a child; the rod of discipline will remove it far from him." Both tools—instruction and discipline—are mentioned in Proverbs 19:20, "Listen to counsel and receive discipline, that you may be wise in the end of your days."

I am so grateful for my father in this regard. He presented an example of self-discipline and provided me with the parental discipline I needed. That discipline included spankings—many more than I wanted. But my father's discipline did more to prepare me for the ministry than anything else. He instilled in me habits of self-control and hard work that have served me well.

I can never remember turning around after a spanking and saying, "Thanks, Dad, for that fresh evidence of your love." But every day I see people lacking in discipline, and I'm reminded that I got it from a father who had no initial desire for me to be in ministry (he was not a believer at that time). Yet it was my father who imparted to me the discipline necessary to survive in ministry. In the same way, young moms must have a biblical view of discipline, and understand how the Lord disciplines us (Hebrews 12). When the need for discipline arises they are better prepared to correct and direct their child in the ways of the Lord.

Develop biblical habits for your home. In Deuteronomy 6:8-9, Moses writes, "You shall bind them as a sign on your hand, and they shall be as phylacteries between your eyes. You shall write them on the doorposts of your house and on your gates."

The home is where habits are formed. That's exactly what Moses is saying: "I want you to take the truth of God's Word and bind it on your hands." That symbolizes the Word of God controlling your actions. Everything you do should be dominated by God's truth.

He also says, "I want you to place it on your forehead, between your eyes." That symbolizes the Word of God controlling all your thoughts as well as what you see—your attitudes, values and influences. God also told His people to place the Word of God on the doorposts of their homes and on the gates, which meant to live it out in front of their neighbors and in the marketplace. Your testimony is for all to see.

What are some biblical habits you can display in your home and share with your children? What are some habits that young single women need to develop now, to become the godly women they long to be?

Let me share a few biblical habits I pursued in my home that are sometimes missing today:

1. Pray and read your Bible everyday
2. Obey God no matter what
3. Always tell the truth
4. Always keep your word
5. Serve other people
6. Finish what you start
7. Give it all you've got
8. Use money wisely
9. Always work hard and do your best
10. Seek the wisdom of godly people

You can add the strengths of each dad and mom in any particular home to this list. You have been made and matured by God in a unique way, and those strengths and lessons should be passed on to your children.

THE PRIVILEGE OF LOVING CHILDREN

A great biblical truth that helps young married women to love and like their children (as well as single women who care for children) is that children are a gift from God for the purpose of advancing His kingdom in the world. Psalm 127:3-5 says,

> *Behold, children are an inheritance of Yahweh,*
> *The fruit of the womb is a reward.*
> *Like arrows in the hand of a warrior,*
> *So are the children of one's youth.*
> *How blessed is the man who fills his quiver with them;*
> *They will not be ashamed*
> *When they speak with enemies in the gate.*

God says that children are a reward for wanting to please and serve Him. We know that's what He means because the Psalm talks about children being weapons and allies in our spiritual warfare. They are not given to us primarily to make us feel good, but to bring glory to God.

That will keep you from asking, "Lord, why did You give me this kid?" The first child is born; no problems. You say, "Jump," and he says, "How high?" The first child conforms. The second one comes along, and this one is "the beast of parental nightmares." Everything that worked with the first child does not work with the second. You say, "Lord, what happened?" His answer: "Nothing. I'm just trying to make you more like Me."

"The gift of children also serves as a way to make you more like Christ."

Many believers think that God only gives us children because of what we can do for them. But that's only a part of the Lord's design. The gift of children also serves as a way to make you more like Christ. It is impossible to raise godly children without recognizing your dependence upon the Lord. The pursuit of godly parenting will have a tremendous impact on your spiritual growth.

FOR SINGLE WOMEN

What you just read is not only true for married women, but also for single women. Here are some practical steps you can take now to prepare you for motherhood later, if the Lord wills.

Build a relationship with a family that has young children. Become a favorite auntie to those kids. Learn from the experiences of those parents. Identify the kids' strengths and weaknesses and work at liking, serving and investing in them as part of your ministry.

Learn to express love to all children. Train yourself to brighten up when you see them, give them your full attention, hug them. Learn how to play with kids.

Pray that God would teach you to appreciate, understand and honor the role of a mother.

Look for opportunities to assist women in handling their children during moments of stress. Develop these skills now in preparation for later.

When praying for your husband-to-be, don't only pray that he'll be a Spirit-filled Christian, but also pray that he will grow to be a great husband and father. Pray for a husband who will lead the family and disciple your future children.

As this chapter concludes, I want to remind you of the simple truth that to become a true lover of children, you have to first become like a child. Luke 18:15-17 says, "And they were bringing even their babies to Him so that He would touch them, but when the disciples saw it, they were rebuking them. But Jesus called for them, saying, 'Permit the children to come to Me, and do not hinder them, for the kingdom of God belongs to such as these. Truly I say to you, whoever does not receive the kingdom of God like a child will never enter it.'"

Jesus loves children. The only way you can truly love children the same way as Christ, is to have the Lord living inside of you. You need to come to Him with the trust of a child, believing He died for your sins, rose from the dead and is the only way for salvation. Repent and ask Christ to give you a new heart. A born again heart desires to obey God's Word more than obeying today's cultural ideas of motherhood. Like a child who needs to be rescued, cry out to your Heavenly Father for salvation. Then ask Him for the strength to be the woman He designed you to be.

FOR PERSONAL REFLECTION & GROUP DISCUSSION:

1. When have you experienced children being lovable and unlovable?

2. What are some ways you see the world's opposition toward having and raising children?

3. What is your picture of an ideal mother? Is that consistent with the way the Bible describes a mother?

4. What are some areas of growth for you in becoming a better mom, or preparing to be a future mom?

5. Ask an older godly woman how she has grown spiritually as a result of being a mother.

6

LET THE WOMEN BE SENSIBLE

A GODLY WOMAN OF SOUND MIND

"Be of sober spirit, be watchful. Your adversary, the devil, prowls around like a roaring lion, seeking someone to devour."

1 PETER 5:8

Nearly every group in our culture is pressuring women to live according to worldly standards.

Consider the world of high fashion. It tells women that to be accepted and beautiful, they must look like a model. Since models represent less than one percent of the women in the world, this causes serious anxiety with the other 99 percent. The cosmetic and clothing industries generate billions of dollars, based on impossible worldly standards. Additionally, women all over the world spend billions on medical procedures like Botox, liposuction, implants, and other plastic surgeries.

The women's liberation movement promotes the idea that the perfect man has an effeminate side and will stay home and care for the kids so that his wife can be a lawyer, business executive, or fight in the military. This pattern of thinking creates role confusion within a marriage.

Taking the unisex philosophy to its farthest extreme, the LGBTQ+ movement loudly promotes the idea that true male and female roles do not exist. Many states have bowed to their pressure and now include "non-binary" on birth certificates. This movement says we must evaluate our position in society by its ever-changing criteria—whether you are straight, gay, transgender or an increasing number of divergent categories.

"The majority of young men and women have never seen a husband and wife follow God's design."

Add to that the present statistics on divorce in the U.S. and it's no wonder that so many men and women are confused about their roles in marriage. Many today have not seen how attractive a biblical marriage can be. The majority of young men and women have never seen a husband and wife follow God's design. When children have only known fighting, conflict and divorce as their marriage model, it produces heartbreak, frustration and failure. Children then grow into teens, collegians and single adults who can't figure out what a man or woman is supposed to be.

Because this world is hostile toward God, what these young women hear is how out of date the Bible is concerning His design for them. This is why it is essential to have older godly women model sensibility. God's children must recognize and reject the distorted ideas being proclaimed as normal by our culture today.

In an interview in Rolling Stone Magazine, Cyndi Lauper—the orange-headed 80's pop star who sang "Girls Just Want to Have Fun"—defined the problem from the world's viewpoint.

Lauper said that the three biggest oppressors of women are the government, the family and the church. She targets three God ordained institutions, clearly showing whose side she is on. As a Christian, you must realize that the role of women is not just a cultural, political, sociological or sexist issue—no, the role of women is a biblical issue.

Chauvinism and feminism are both wrong—only God's perspective is right. God is the One who made male and female, and He gave each gender specific functions to pursue. As His child, it's essential you understand and follow God's divine blueprint outlined in the Bible. Otherwise, you will find yourself constantly confused and competing with the opposite sex.

It's tough today for women of any age to figure out how to fulfill their roles. Consider the challenges for a young single woman today:

- If she waits to marry, she will probably be seen as desperate.
- If she pursues a career, it will be hard to give it up when she gets married or starts having kids.
- If she focuses on her deep desire to be a wife and mother by reading every book she can find on the subject to prepare, she'll easily become frustrated by not being able to apply what she is studying.
- Even if she is content with her singleness, that won't stop her family and friends from asking her five times each week, "When are you going to get married?"
- If she pursues ministry, she fears that she will become so spiritual that she will be intimidating to the men around her or so out-of-circulation that she will never meet anyone.

So, what is a single Christian woman to do in this modern era?

UNDERSTANDING SENSIBILITY

In Titus, the third character quality listed is a key to all the others—perhaps that's why it's mentioned right after loving husbands and children. What should be the overriding attribute of the Christian woman's mind? What should family and others in your life conclude when they evaluate how you think? One word will describe the mind of the godly woman—sensible.

We have all known women who are so self-focused that they could be described as narcissistic, neurotic, or paranoid—she suffers from the disease of ingrown eyeballs. There are women shopaholics who continually overspend and live constantly in debt. Some single women may fall for the first guy who gives her his attention. There are singles who invest more time on their physical appearance than they do developing a heart for the Lord. Some young women spend more of their life trending on social media than they do pursuing godliness. If any of that describes you, even just a little, then you need to learn how to develop sensibility.

In order to hit a target, you have to know what the target looks like. What does Paul mean when he says young women are to be sensible?

BIBLICAL DESCRIPTIONS OF A SENSIBLE WOMAN

In the New Testament a sensible woman possesses the combination of three qualities, as we learn from other uses of the Greek word.

First, she is in her **right mind**. The Greek word for "sensible" (sophronas) is used this way in Luke 8:35: "And the people went out to see what had happened, and they came to Jesus, and found the man from whom the demons had gone out, sitting down at the feet of Jesus, clothed and in his right mind [that's the word for 'sensible']." You may not be demon possessed, but you can still be influenced by worldly wisdom which the Bible describes as demonic (James 3:15).

Next, a sensible woman is **calm**. 1 Peter 4:7: "The end of all things is at hand; therefore, be of sound thinking [that's the word for 'sensible'] and sober spirit for the purpose of prayer."

A sensible woman rarely panics, becomes enraged, or otherwise loses control over her emotions. Instead she thinks things through and prays about everything.

Finally, she uses **common sense**. Paul says in Romans 12:3, "Think so as to have sound thinking [that's the word for 'sensible'] as God has allotted to each a measure of faith." A sensible woman makes Christ-honoring decisions based on the Word of God, and even applies biblical wisdom on issues that the Bible does not directly address.

"In other words, the sensible woman is a thinking woman. She is morally alert."

In other words, the sensible woman is a thinking woman. She is morally alert. She avoids watching or reading anything impure. When dating she avoids being alone with a man in the dark or out late, because she understands sexual drives. She avoids extremes in her behavior. She exercises restraint in her speech, and she thinks before she acts. As Proverbs 14:16 says, "A wise man fears and turns away from evil, but a fool gets angry and feels secure."

The Bible not only calls young women to live sensibly here in Titus 2, but the Scripture as a whole uses words similar to sensibility, which give us a clearer picture of this important attribute.

One word is **discretion**, which means to show good judgment and display discernment in one's lifestyle. Toddlers lack this quality. That's why they will call any four-legged animal a "doggie"—a cow is a "doggie," a horse is a "doggie," a pig is a "doggie." Likewise, a single woman who lacks discretion will consider attention from a handsome male as love, even though it might be lust, friendship or merely Christian concern. But a woman with discretion evaluates everything based on the Word of God, desiring to see all of life through God's eyes.

Another similar Greek word is **temperate**, which means moderation, not only regarding the use of alcohol but also many other issues. A temperate life is bound within self-imposed limitations. It avoids extremes and excesses. A junior high girl who is not temperate might start drinking alcohol just because her friends do. The young woman who is not temperate might respond to a man who says he loves her, by giving herself physically to him. Some women indulge in endless media binges to escape their problems. Anyone lacking temperance might eat an entire carton of ice cream in one sitting, or an entire box of chocolates because of a big disappointment. But a woman who is temperate will avoid such extremes in her behavior.

Lastly, self-controlled means "able to sacrifice immediate pleasures to secure ultimate purposes." **Self-control** is making the choice to follow the Word of God over any other commitments, goals, schools of thought, or friends. The sensible person can show restraint over his or her own impulses, emotions, urges, and desires.

A single woman who lacks self-control will not be able to say no to emotional or sexual desires for greater intimacy and will compromise her values. A woman without self-control will not take her thoughts captive to truth (2 Corinthians 10:5) but will allow herself to believe lies and think depressing thoughts.

"...a woman with self-control will sacrifice immediate gratification in order to honor God."

She will allow her emotions to dominate her world. But a woman with self-control will sacrifice immediate gratification in order to honor God. A Christian's sensibility empowered by the Holy Spirit provides discernment, control and balance.

THE IMPORTANCE OF SENSIBILITY

Sensibility is the most repeated quality in the book of Titus. The Christians on Crete were having difficulty living what they believed because their culture encouraged senseless living. Titus 1:12-14 states, "One of themselves, a prophet of their own, said, 'Cretans are always liars, evil beasts, lazy gluttons.' This testimony is true. For this reason reprove them severely so that they may be sound in the faith, not paying attention to Jewish myths and commandments of men who turn away from the truth."

Notice Paul says it is true that Cretans are always liars, meaning they exercise no control over their speech. They are evil beasts, meaning they manifest wild, uncontrollable, senseless behavior. And they are lazy gluttons, having no control over their appetites.

Notice also in verse 14 that they pay attention to myths and tickle their ears with men's opinions. They allow their minds to be entertained with things that are not sensible instead of letting the Word of God control their lives by yielding to the Spirit of God.

Crete was like our society is today—if it feels good do it, indulge yourself, abandon your inhibitions and seek pleasure. Our culture encourages living without sensibility. Paul makes sensibility the number-one character quality for Titus to model and teach, and no doubt he would say the same thing for us today.

One example of Paul's repeated pleas for sensibility is in Titus 2:11-12: "For the grace of God has appeared, bringing salvation to all men, instructing us that, denying ungodliness and worldly desires, we should live sensibly, righteously and godly in the present age." Sensibility is essential—and the consequences of not having it are devastating.

The Bible says that without sensibility, even a beautiful woman will look unattractive. Proverbs 11:22 says, "As a ring of gold in a swine's snout, so is a beautiful woman who turns away from discretion." What a picture! A beautiful gold ornament would become filthy in the snout of a pig; it would be an object of disgust instead of beauty. And God's Word says that's what happens to a gorgeous woman who lacks sensible discretion—she becomes an object of disgust.

"She strategizes how to live a God-honoring life."

On the other hand, a person with sensibility has the ability to count the cost in every situation. This person is like the builder who takes serious consideration before he builds a tower, and like the king who has a serious discussion with his advisors before going to battle against a larger army (Luke 14:28-32). The sensible woman thinks before she acts. She is the one who plans ahead before shopping. She methodically organizes her home, her finances and her life. She strategizes how to live a God-honoring life. She carefully considers her life goals and education. She prayerfully considers relationships and marriage. She guards her affections and emotions. She diligently pursues her spiritual life.

In the book of Titus, God is telling you to take sensibility seriously. Sensibility is a crucial habit to develop so that you can withstand the real tests that bombard you from our ungodly society and the stress of everyday circumstances and relationships.

WHAT SENSIBILITY LOOKS LIKE

A sensible young woman will be radically different from the world in her thinking, emotion, appearance and spending. Let's take a closer look at each of those important areas, so young women and the older women who mentor them will know how to practically live out this godly characteristic.

"No one can be a healthy Christian without healthy thoughts."

IN YOUR THOUGHTS

No one can be a healthy Christian without healthy thoughts. People say "you are what you eat"—but God's Word says you are what you think: "For as he calculates in his soul, so he is" (Proverbs 23:7). God's Word tells you what Christ wants you to think about: "Finally, brothers, whatever is true, whatever is dignified, whatever is right, whatever is pure, whatever is lovely, whatever is commendable, if there is any excellence and if anything worthy of praise, consider these things" (Philippians 4:8).

You have to work at this, but the sensible woman has learned that much of what she thinks is a matter of choice. Bad thoughts will fly through your mind, but Christians can choose whether or not those thoughts will land and be pondered further. Temptations will come, but you do not have to dwell on them. As Martin Luther liked to say, "You can't stop the birds from flying overhead, but you don't have to let them build a nest in your hair."

So, how can you keep bad thoughts from nesting in your mind? 2 Corinthians 10:5 talks about refusing to embrace false philosophies but it can also be used to address thinking, when Paul says, "Take every thought captive to the obedience of Christ."

Practically, you should say something like this when sinful thoughts come to mind: *No, that thinking is wrong! It is not true. It is in contradiction to Your Word, Lord. It is not pleasing to You and does not promote Your glory. Oh, Lord, I want to obey you, and turn the focus of my thoughts to You and Your truth.* You can't dwell on wrong thoughts and focus on the Lord at the same time.

A sensible person realizes that spiritual health depends on biblical thinking. Thoughts are the key to being filled with the Spirit, living obediently, overcoming temptation and growing in spiritual maturity. So the godly young Christian woman will work at keeping her thoughts healthy.

IN YOUR EMOTIONS

How do you know if your emotions are getting the best of you? Ask yourself these key questions – if you answer "yes" to any of them, you have a problem with your emotions:

- Do I often spend money because of an advertisement?
- Do I dwell on my hurts for hours?
- Do I worry about what people think of me?
- Do I get consumed with celebrities or other people's lives?
- Do I battle with feeling sorry for myself?

The Bible gives instruction about controlling, guiding and directing your emotions. For example, Proverbs 29:11 says, "A fool lets out all of his spirit, but a wise man holds it back." And Ephesians 4:26 says, "Be angry, and yet do not sin; do not let the sun go down on your anger." A sensible woman will not let her emotions overrule her reason. The following are biblical principles for controlling your feelings.

Start by being honest about your emotions. Ecclesiastes 3:4 says, "[There is] a time to weep and a time to laugh; a time to mourn and a time to dance." 1 Corinthians 12:25-26 admonishes us to be genuine and compassionate towards brothers and sisters in the body of Christ: "The members [should] have the same care for one another. And if one member suffers, all the members suffer with it; if one member is honored, all the members rejoice with it." Talk to God about how you feel, about what is going on in your heart. But don't stop there.

Be responsible for your emotions. Proverbs 16:2-3 says, "All the ways of a man are pure in his own sight, but Yahweh weighs the motives. Commit your works to Yahweh and your plans will be established."

Ask yourself if your emotions are drawing you closer to Christ or pushing you farther away. Are they reflective of a pure heart or of one divided by mixed motives? Are you taking your thoughts captive to obedience to Christ?

There is a desperate need for emotional control today, especially among single women. Too many single women allow their emotions to deceive them. They tell themselves that the man they love will change, or that he'll find Christ, or that he'll become a leader—but their emotions are only deceiving them. All the while, their conscience is signaling warnings to get out before it's too late.

Sensibility demands you never give your emotions or your heart away to a young man unless his character meets these basic essentials:

- He is a genuine believer—fruitful and faithful.
- He is a Spirit-filled Christian, who strives to become more like Christ.
- He is a man who is masculine in the ways defined by the Word.
- He is a man who consistently seeks God's plan for his life.
- He is a man of good reputation in the church, the community and those who know him.

The sensible woman guards her heart and is very careful about the one she becomes attached to. She is not one who gets a little attention from a guy and then gives him her heart's devotion. How do you recognize a woman who has failed to guard her heart in a relationship? It's the one who is devastated and crushed after a breakup. Or she is guilt-ridden and aloof after the relationship is over. It's the young woman who gets connected to a guy, and then disappears from her friends, her church and her parents to pursue this man.

Now is the time for young single women to develop convictions about how to guard their heart. Here are four important considerations:

1. Be careful about how much time you spend together.
2. Be careful about the gifts you give and receive.
3. Be careful about the promises that are made.
4. Be careful about the speed of the relationship.

Think about what is sensible at the beginning of any dating relationship. Is spending four hours a week or spending 24 hours a week a sensible amount of time? Is a gift of flowers or a diamond ring sensible? Is it sensible to promise spending the rest of your life together after only dating a week? Is accepting a marriage proposal after three dates a sensible speed in any relationship?

"The main reason for the attraction between you and your date should not be how you feel or the way he looks. It should be that he is a godly Christian—a man of the Word and prayer..."

The main reason for the attraction between you and your date should not be how you feel or the way he looks. It should be that he is a godly Christian—a man of the Word and prayer, a man of character and faithful service in the local church. This makes him one who is worthy of your trust and respect. Sensibility means both you and your young man avoid saying "I love you" without being able to back it up like Christ did, with your whole life. Never allow him to promise anything until he can promise everything.

IN YOUR APPEARANCE

In 1 Timothy 2:9 God says, "I want women to adorn themselves with proper clothing, with modesty and self-restraint." The sensible young woman considers her dressing habits. Be aware, ladies: not only does your dress reveal your character, but it can send some very loud and clear messages. The sensible woman is careful about not only the intended messages of her appearance, but also the messages that might be misinterpreted because of it.

The harsh reality is that you may wear certain clothes with the intention of looking attractive and making a positive impression, but the message received by men is that you are sexually available. I read a survey once that most junior high boys believe that the message girls are sending by wearing tight jeans is a desire for sexual activity.

Recently, I was walking behind a woman at a local sports arena. She must have sprayed her top and pants on, they were so tight and revealing. Instead of watching her, I watched the men coming from the other direction. Without exception, they all stared at her, and one man even made an obscene comment.

No matter what the commercials say, it's not a good thing to dress provocatively in public. If you're not trying to seduce or get sexual attention from men, but you dress immodestly, you are revealing an ignorance of both the depravity of man and the physical drive inherent in men. Men in general are beasts, and even Christian men can act beastly. Just as you are seeking to grow more mature in Christ with your thinking and emotions, so most young men are still in the process of learning to control their sexual desires. They are responsible for their drives and desires, but you are responsible for creating temptation by what you wear.

You are not responsible for some pervert's thought-life but you are responsible for the message of your clothing choices. Sensible living means thinking about the message you want to send with your clothing choices, and also thinking about what messages could be received by others. Part of the reason it is crucial to be trained by older Godly women is to work through exactly what kind of signals you are sending by how you behave and by what you wear.

IN YOUR SPENDING

Proverbs 15:16 says, "Better is a little with the fear of Yahweh than great treasure and turmoil with it." Matthew 6:19-21 says,

> *Do not store up for yourselves treasures on earth, where moth and rust destroy, and where thieves break in and steal. But store up for yourselves treasures in heaven, where neither moth nor rust destroys, and where thieves do not break in or steal; for where your treasure is, there your heart will be also.*

Luke 16:11 says, "if you have not been faithful in the use of unrighteous wealth, who will entrust the true riches to you?"

Are you faithful with money? Are you investing in heaven? What does your bank statement say about your heart? Are you trying to serve Christ and have it all too? Be sensible with your resources.

Whatever you do, don't develop a habit of spending what you don't have and going into debt. Not only is that sin, but you're also sowing the seeds of destruction for your current or future marriage, since one of the top marital problems is money.

Don't be like the young wife who was struggling with her finances and agreed with her husband that whenever they were tempted to make an impulsive purchase, they would say, "Get behind me, Satan." This worked great until one evening, the wife brought home an expensive new dress that obviously was not a necessity. Her husband asked her if she forgot to say, "Get behind me, Satan." She said, "No, I said it." "Then what happened?" the husband asked, and she confessed, "Satan said, 'It looks good from the back too!'"

Learn to make a budget and use it. Be sensible about your

spending habits. Evaluate why you want to buy things. Don't use credit cards unless you already have the money to pay off the bill. Use cash for your spending money—not your credit card. Then, once your cash is gone, you will not spend any more. Remember that your money actually belongs to Christ, not you, so figure out how you can save it, invest it and spend it in a way which would honor Him best.

HOW TO GROW IN SENSIBILITY

A good place to start is to always check your motives. Make a lifetime habit of asking yourself, *What is my motive?*—in relationships, conversations, dress, and all life choices. Is everything you do done in the power of the Spirit, according to the Word of God, and for Christ's glory? Know that God will only ever reward those things done for His glory and in the power of the Spirit. Sensibility only comes as life is lived dependent upon Christ—not relying on human feelings, ideas, or opinions, but on the Spirit of Truth and the Word of Truth.

Next, be faithful in the Christian disciplines. Develop habits of prayer, Bible study, fellowship, worship and service. In our day, it's popular to have a self-defined god or a personalized, independent faith, where people think…

- I made a profession of faith, so I'm saved.
- I can do what I want and still be saved.
- I can attend church sporadically, read the Bible once in a while, fellowship when it's convenient, never give, never serve and still be a mature believer.

This kind of Christianity is self-defined, not God defined. It is a faith made up in your head rather than revealed by God in His Word. When you live that way, you're like a piece of a jigsaw puzzle trying to make it out on your own. You've made up your own idea of where you fit or don't fit, all the time denying you belong with all the other parts of the puzzle. You're standing all alone outside of

God's plan, or you're trying to force yourself to fit somewhere you don't belong. An independent, self-defined believer is only living for themself and not Christ.

When Christ is truly your Savior, He is also Lord of your life (Matthew 7:21, Luke 6:46). When you are saved, Christ gives you a new heart that wants to obey, pray, read the Bible, grow in a local church community, minister your gifts, share the gospel, give sacrificially and worship corporately.

A sensible Christian seeks to pursue all these disciplines of the Christian life—they are the means by which we experience God's grace and growth in our lives. Don't commit to these disciplines out of an ambition to become a super Christian, but because it will strengthen the intimacy you have with Christ and bring Him glory.

Thirdly, pray for godly mentors. In order to live these character qualities, women must be trained in them by older godly women. The best way this happens is in the context of local church ministry.

By now you should know, ladies, this is not optional. In addition to your mom (if she is a mature Christian), seek out some other older godly woman (or a group of women). Even with the Holy Spirit and the Word of God to guide you, you still need the help of other women to identify and practice sensibility. In the context of a biblical mentoring relationship, these older women are the ones who can give godly counsel, properly evaluate your life, protect you from pitfalls and keep you from error.

Finally, develop a teachable heart. To become sensible, you must be teachable.

Proverbs 12:15 says, "The way of an ignorant fool is right in his own eyes, but a wise man is he who listens to counsel." Young women must ask questions, be eager to learn, and be willing to follow the wisdom and example of older women.

FOR PERSONAL REFLECTION & GROUP DISCUSSION:

1. What foolish beliefs are prevalent among women today who are considered "wise"? Why do you think those ideas are so popular?

2. Why is the way you think important for your spiritual life? (Romans 12:2 and Ephesians 4:23)

3. How can you "take every thought captive to the obedience of Christ?" What does that mean in specific and practical terms?

4. Make a list of your standards for modesty. Ask a godly older woman to review it and provide input.

5. Being sensible requires a teachable heart. How willing are you to learn from Scripture and godly mentors?

7

LET THE WOMEN BE PURE

A GODLY WOMAN IS PURE

"But the goal of our command is love from a pure heart and a good conscience and an unhypocritical faith."

1 TIMOTHY 1:5

Back in ancient times, one of the Near Eastern cultures had an interesting way of punishing murderers. Those assigned to carry out justice would bind together the bodies of the murdered man and his murderer. They would force the mouths of both open, and then bind their heads together mouth to mouth. It would look like the murderer was giving his dead victim mouth-to-mouth resuscitation.

The murderer might live for days with his victim forcibly attached to him, but eventually all the impurities from the decaying dead man would migrate into the murderer and cause his death. The reasoning behind this form of punishment was that justice was satisfied because the murdered man killed his murderer.

This punishment seems gross and barbaric. But spiritually,

a similar idea is happening in the Christian community today. Just look around you—you'll see Christians bound up and going mouth-to-mouth with a dead world system. Christians ingest all kinds of impurities that damage their spiritual lives and bring about pain and anguish for the rest of their lives. This love affair with the world is so widespread among Christians today that true purity has become the rare exception rather than the rule. But it's crucial for every Christian, whether married or single, to know what God says about purity—and specifically about sexual purity.

Everyone battles with physical purity to some degree. Many of you experience guilt over past sins—what you did before you were born again or before you were married. Many experience problems in marriage linked to sexual guilt over what you see on the internet or in the entertainment you watch. Guilt can grow due to an impure thought life, masturbation or compromises that have been made. Your only real hope for these problems is God's grace in salvation and God's Word in sanctification. That gives you the help you need to keep a clean conscience and maintain a pure heart.

The topic of sexual purity is not merely important—it's crucial. Paul mentions it as a part of his list of essential qualities for young women in Titus 2:4-5: "Instruct the young women…to be…pure… so that the Word of God will not be slandered."

In order for the church to be an effective witness for Jesus Christ, women must be morally pure. The word "pure" is used this way eight times in the New Testament. For example, 1 Timothy 5:22 says, "keep yourself pure," and 1 Peter 3:2 says, "as they observe your pure conduct with fear."

God calls you to be sexually pure in your heart and life. This was a problem in the first century, and it is a problem today, even for Christians. Why? Because we ignore or belittle our owner's manual, the inspired Word of God.

When I bought my little Honda, I received an owner's manual. That book gives me instructions on how to operate my car. It tells me how to put gas in the gas tank, oil in the engine and water in the radiator. What if I were to treat my car owner's manual in the way that most Christians treat their owner's manual, the Bible? I would buy a lie and say, "Honda Motor Company is just trying to ruin my enjoyment of this car by giving me all these arbitrary rules to follow. I think I'll put water in the gas tank because it is cheaper than gas. Oil is so sticky—I think I'll put water in the engine too. The radiator is always leaking, so I won't put anything in there." If I did that, my car would be headed for serious trouble. And so are those Christians who ignore God's Word in the matter of purity.

Why do so many Christians fail in this area of life? Because they disregard the clear and practical principles in the Bible, their owner's manual. They forget that following instructions from the Word of God is vital for friendships, relationships, engagement, marriage and family to bring God glory and be a blessing to us. God meant those instructions not only to bring Him glory, but also for our good and happiness. Your Heavenly Father loves you. There is an unbreakable bond between you and the Lord. Your Father wants what is best for you and that is moral purity.

"Your Heavenly Father loves you. There is an unbreakable bond between you and the Lord. Your Father wants what is best for you and that is moral purity."

It was God who created and designed men and women—not Hollywood, higher education, the government or any other human authority. Only God is the true authority on how people should believe and behave. The only way a woman will be truly happy and blessed is to turn from her sin to follow Christ as Lord, depend on the Holy Spirit and follow the Bible as the only pattern for her life.

So let's look at sexual purity from God's perspective and how to develop godly purity in our lives.

GOD'S DESIGN FOR SEXUAL INTIMACY

Biblically, sexual intimacy includes all the thoughts, drives, emotions and actions leading up to and including sexual intercourse. It is not merely the final act, but everything leading up to it. So what did God design sexual intimacy to be?

WITHIN THE CONTEXT OF MARRIAGE

First, God made sexual intimacy for a man and a woman. God designed sex to be between a male and a female. When God created the human race, he created Adam and Eve, not Adam and Steve. It was God who created sex, not the porn industry. In Genesis 2:18, God says, "It is not good for the man to be alone," so He created the woman. And in Genesis 2:24, He exhorts them to leave, to cleave and to become one flesh. Becoming one flesh is the consummation of their commitment. It goes beyond the physical union—it's a total joining in every area of their lives. Notice the order—leave, then cleave, then lastly, one flesh. The physical is last. God designed this intimacy between a man and a woman with one of the purposes being to have children.

Second, God made sexual intimacy for marriage. Over 25 times in the Bible God says sexual intimacy outside of marriage is a sin. But Hebrews 13:4 says that inside of marriage, sexual intimacy is honorable. In marriage, God gives His joyous approval to sexual intimacy because He is the One who designed the perfect program.

Lastly, sexual intimacy in marriage is for the enjoyment of the other partner. In 1 Corinthians 7:1-5 Paul says that in marriage the wife's body does not belong to her but to her husband, and the husband's body belongs to the wife. They are for each other, not for themselves. You gave yourself to your spouse when you said, "I do."

This explains why masturbation is sinful. Sex in marriage is not merely for your own pleasure or to cure lust. It is for the enjoyment of the other partner. God provides sex as a gift and blessing within marriage, but we must follow His design.

OUTSIDE OF MARRIAGE

Let's look at what Scripture says about sexual purity for singles. Consider these two questions.

First, at what point is physical touch wrong between a woman and a man who are not married? Typically, singles try to manage the physical aspect of relationships by drawing a line—no more than holding hands, or stop hugging or never kiss. But physical touch outside of marriage should be governed by God's standard, and 1 Corinthians 7:1-2 answers the question by saying, "It is good for a man not to touch a woman. But because of sexual immoralities, each man is to have his own wife, and each woman is to have her own husband."

What does Paul mean by "touch?" The word is used several times in the Bible to mean non-sexual touch, but the context here implies that the usage in this verse is referring to the whole process of sexual intimacy outside of marriage—which God calls immorality. In other words, it is good for a man not to touch a woman in such a way as to stir up sensual desires, ultimately leading to sexual intercourse. It implies everything that leads up to that final act.

Does that mean you can't hold hands? Maybe. You mean you can't hug? That depends. Kiss? Only if you don't stir up any desires. This is God's standard for the single. You should never be responsible for anyone being turned-on sexually.

Now, why would God give us such a general principle? Why wasn't He more specific? Because everyone is different. If God drew a specific line for us, we would immediately head for that line. Just imagine if the biblical line was hugs. God would have needed to spell out how long a hug could be before it crosses the line—we'd need a timer to know when we're sinning. God would have had to speak about how tight a godly hug could be—the gentle flower hug is spiritual but the jaws of death hug is not. God would have had to spell out the angle of the hug—side, back, or front?

Instead, God wisely tells us we can touch with natural affection and Christlike care, but once the sexual desires are heating up, you've gone too far. Stay far away from your internal limit, your individual line. God wants you to keep your heart and mind free from lust. If you are single, don't let someone arouse you sexually. And don't do that to anyone else.

The next question to consider is: what's so bad about sexual intimacy outside of marriage? The answer is that sexual intimacy won't satisfy your desires, and it won't solve your problems. Hebrews 11:25 says Moses chose "rather to be mistreated with the people of God than to enjoy the passing pleasures of sin." That passage tells us that sin is often enjoyable or pleasurable. But God says the pleasure of sin is passing, temporary and fleeting. It won't last or satisfy.

We often think that sexual immorality will solve the problems of loneliness and insecurity. We think it will relieve our strong passions, but it does so only temporarily and is accompanied by guilt, fear, anger, more lust and doubt.

God gave you strong drives to enjoy in marriage, but their purpose before marriage is for you to learn self-control. If you don't learn self-control before marriage, you will still struggle with it in various ways after you are married.

1 Corinthians 6 helps us understand why sex outside of marriage is wrong. Paul says in verse 12, "All things are lawful for me, but not all things are profitable. All things are lawful for me, but I will not be mastered by anything." Sexual sin will master you. If an unmarried couple allows premarital sex to enter

their relationship, it will become the priority. They will disappear from fellowship because they are enslaved to lust through sexual involvement.

Sexual sin is also in opposition to the purpose of our bodies. In 1 Corinthians 6:13 Paul says, "Food is for the stomach and the stomach is for food, but God will do away with both of them. Yet the body is not for sexual immorality, but for the Lord, and the Lord is for the body." The purpose of your body is to reflect the glory of God. Our body is for Him. As verse 20 says, "You were bought with a price: therefore glorify God in your body." Your body is not to reflect impurity, but rather purity because God is pure.

Sexual sin is also "against our bodies." It's not just against your body's purpose, but actually against your body itself. 1 Corinthians 6:18 says, "Flee sexual immorality. Every other sin that a man commits is outside the body, but the sexually immoral man sins against his own body." Do you realize, Christian, that if you lie, you can correct it by telling the truth. If you steal, you can give back what you stole. But if you have pre-marital sex, you can never give back what you took. Nor can you recover what you lost. Your virginity is a gift that is only given away once. God intended your body to be a gift to your spouse on your wedding day.

Wake up to the fact that sexual sin will permanently scar your life. It is a sin that can be forgiven, completely and totally in Christ. However, it is a sin that you will sadly never forget and others won't either.

"Sexual sin is also to be avoided because it involves God in your sin."

Sexual sin is also to be avoided because it involves God in your sin. 1 Corinthians 6:16-17 says, "Do you not know that the one who joins himself to a prostitute is one body with her? For He says,

'The two shall become one flesh.' But the one who joins himself to the Lord is one spirit with Him." No Christian would ever show a pornographic movie to their church elders, yet there are many calling themselves Christians who expose the Holy Spirit of God to fornication, using their bodies to commit sexual sin in His presence.

Sexual sin is against a body we don't own. Remember verse 20: "You were bought with a price: therefore glorify God in your body." Your body is not your own. Your body is God's body; therefore it should be used to honor Him.

FLEE IMMORALITY

The issue in our minds should never be how much we can get away with physically or how close we can get to sin without actually sinning. Our focus should be on how close we can get to Christ and how far we can stay away from sin. The goal should be to honor God through our bodies, sexually and otherwise.

Remember, Christians are commanded to "flee immorality." Sex outside of marriage, impure sexual thoughts or any defilement from the world should cause the Christian to run away. Flee that situation as fast as you can and never subject yourself to a situation like that again. Look at 1 Corinthians 6:18 again: "Flee sexual immorality. Every other sin that a man commits is outside the body, but the sexually immoral man sins against his own body."

Not only is the verb "flee" a command to literally run in terror, it is also a continual fleeing. That means the Christian is to have a lifestyle that continually runs from immorality, impurity, and lust. On every date and in every relationship, the Christian is to guard themself from sexual sin and run away if necessary.

God has clearly commanded his children to not sin sexually in 1 Thessalonians 4:2-3: "For you know what commandments we gave you through the Lord Jesus. For this is the will of God, your sanctification [your purity]: that you abstain from sexual immorality." The Greek word for "abstain" means "to hold oneself from." The word for "sexual immorality" includes any and all sexual sin. Christians are commanded by God to stay away from any sexual sin, from lustful thoughts to premartial or extramarital sex.

When you commit sexual sin with another person, it is not only against God or your own body, but also against your sexual partner and others. It is a sin against your spouse or future spouse and also your sexual partner's spouse or future spouse.

DON'T DEFRAUD OR BE DEFRAUDED

Look at 1 Thessalonians 4:6-8:

> *No man [should] transgress and defraud his brother in the matter because the Lord is the avenger in all these things, just as we also told you before and solemnly warned you. For God did not call us to impurity, but in sanctification. Consequently, he who sets this aside is not setting aside man but the God who gives His Holy Spirit to you.*

When Paul says in verse 6 that we're not to transgress, he means we are not to go beyond, exceed the limits or violate the rights of another. Transgressing or "defrauding" is to selfishly gain something at someone else's expense—literally cheating or deceiving someone out of their purity.

Practically, our words should never promise anything before marriage that God only intended within marriage. For example, saying, "I love you" in order to open the door for physical intimacy. Our actions should never cause physical arousal to the point of lust.

What is lust? Most of the New Testament occurrences of the word refer to strong desires in opposition to God's Word. When you lust, you sin; when you cause others to lust, you defraud them, which is also sin. If you continue to sin against others in this way, verse 6 says God will be "the avenger." Literally, that means that He will carry out a sentence against you.

There are many reasons to stay pure, but a simple one to motivate you is that God will make you pay. God avenges the wrongs you have done, by disciplining you if you are His child or condemning you forever if you are not. Verse 8 says that by sinning sexually you're rejecting God, you're rejecting the guidance of the Spirit in you and you're rejecting God's holiness.

You can see why God's design for purity is so important. So, why do so many people fail to follow it?

"Purity is such a big problem because Christians easily forget they are in a constant battle against themselves."

DON'T BE DECEIVED BY SEXUAL SIN

Purity is such a big problem because Christians easily forget they are in a constant battle against themselves. Sin deceives us because most of its consequences are hidden. James 1:14 says, "Each one is tempted when he is carried away and enticed by his own lust." Notice the words "carried away" and "enticed." The expression "carried away" evokes the idea of baiting a trap. A hunter leaves a chunk of fresh meat in a trap which is concealed in the snow. There are some immediate rewards for the bear who comes strolling by, because the meat tastes good. All the ugly consequences are hidden from view, but they become all too real for the bear when the inescapable trap is sprung. There is pleasure in sexual sin, but a death trap is hidden underneath its pleasures.

The word "enticed" was used in reference to baiting a hook. Again, it speaks of both immediate gratification and concealment. The fish is promised something appealing without a description of the consequences. Since fish are ignorant of how hooks work, they are caught. They have no idea that suffering and death await them. Similarly, it is easy for us to fantasize about the most exotic sexual experience. But we are blinded to what's happening to ourselves and to others—and particularly to God, Who is grieved by our disobedience.

Believers who enjoy sexual pleasure outside of God's design don't realize they are trapped, and all the while they are getting weaker in conscience and moral strength.

James 1:15-16 explains how people fall into the deception of sexual sin by saying, "Then when lust has conceived, it gives birth to sin, and when sin is fully matured it brings forth death. Do not be deceived." Sin is described here as a process. James says it starts with desire—lust or strong emotions. You think your emotional needs are unmet. Then a person comes into your life who begins to make you feel better. This leads to the next step—deception of the mind. You begin to rationalize your pursuit of your emotional desire. Instead of focusing your thoughts on honoring the Lord, you allow your mind to fantasize about this person and grow emotionally attached.

Emotions kick in first, then thoughts begin to dwell on what you desire. The battle goes from the heart to the mind, and then finally to the will—unless you stop it in the mind.

The emotional responses of "he's handsome" or "he understands me" or "he is so gentle and affectionate" must not be something you dwell on. If you return to these thoughts again and again, your infatuation can lead to sexual sin.

The last step in the deceptive process of sexual sin is physical involvement—enslaving disobedience. If you become emotionally drawn in and allow your mind to build a fantasy, then when circumstances are right, you are likely to fall. When the person responds to us in the way we've fantasized, we are caught in the trap. James 1:15 says, "when lust has conceived..."—once the will is in gear, our thoughts will give birth to sin.

HOW TO DEVELOP SEXUAL PURITY

God has provided a process by which we can grow in purity. Consider a few general principles and some specific methods your Lord has put in place to help you control your drives and desires.

GENERAL PRINCIPLES

First, purity starts with seeking Christ–wanting to love Him, fear Him, and imitate Him. Purity starts with a life that is focused on the only pure One. 1 John 3:2-3 says, "We know that when He is manifested, we will be like Him, because we will see Him just as He is. And everyone who has this hope fixed on Him purifies himself, just as He is pure."

Purity starts not with do's and don'ts, but with Christ. Purity comes from His beauty, His character, His person, His love. If purity does not start with Him—walking daily with Him, learning His Word, living in His presence in all relationships, including marriage—then no amount of rules, laws, or commandments will keep you pure.

A Christianity without Christ is only a bunch of legalistic rules. A Christian lifestyle without the pursuit of Christ can't maintain true purity, because purity only comes from Him. It starts with and continues in Christ Himself. Don't expect to stay pure unless you seek Him with all your heart.

Second, purity starts within. To stay morally clean in a dirty world, you must remember that real purity starts inside your heart. In Mark 7:20-23 Jesus says, "That which proceeds out of the man, that is what defiles the man. For from within, out of the heart of men, proceed the evil thoughts, sexual immoralities, thefts, murders, adulteries, coveting, wickedness, deceit, sensuality, envy, slander, pride and foolishness. All these evil things proceed from within and defile the man." He also says in Matthew 5:27-28, "You have heard that it was said, 'You shall not commit adultery'; but I say to you that everyone who looks at a woman to lust for her has already committed adultery with her in his heart."

Purity also starts with an inner longing to be right with God. There is a true desire to have a clean, guilt-free conscience. Purity is an inner attitude that is lived out in holy behavior.

A cynic may say, "You're judging me; this is legalistic," and they will rationalize excuses. But the pure will say, "I want a clean conscience," and will confess and forsake their sin, refusing to compromise. Proverbs 28:13 says, "He who conceals his transgressions will not prosper, but he who confesses and forsakes them will receive compassion." The pure in heart never allows sin to remain unchecked in his or her life, even when it is only an internal issue.

Finally, purity starts with sensibility. Titus 2:5 indicates that sensibility is necessary in order to live a sexually pure life. That is the sequence of Paul's words—first sensible, then pure. Sensibility is the self-controlled, premeditated planning that enables an individual to deny desires, feelings, drives and passions for the purpose of pleasing Christ.

SPECIFIC METHODS

The Bible's simple instruction for avoiding sexual sin: Flee! 1 Corinthians 6:18 says, "Flee sexual immorality [Run in terror!]," and 2 Timothy 2:22 says, "Flee from youthful lusts."

God doesn't say to fight lust, but to flee lust. God is teaching us that certain sins should not be directly confronted—we must flee them. That means to avoid the situation. If you don't want to get stung, stay away from the bees.

Like Joseph, who knew to run when Potiphar's wife was seducing him, Christians must decide in advance that they'll run when facing sexual temptation. If your boyfriend suddenly shocks you with grabby hands, don't pray about it—run, flee, then dump that guy. If your date is pressuring you to get intimate, don't rationalize it, at that moment, run in terror! Get out of the car, leave the location, call your dad or one of your church leaders.

A better way to prepare for safe dating is to always go out with a mixed group, both male and female friends and don't pair off. Talk about both male and female topics. Learn to be good friends with both sexes. Learn about the opposite sex in a safe atmosphere.

Don't place yourself in situations where you might be tempted. Think before you go to the park or beach at night, alone with your date. Avoid being alone with someone of the opposite sex in an apartment or home. Don't send mixed messages by dressing immodestly or provocatively. Plan ahead to stay in public and open areas to avoid temptation.

Romans 13:14 says, "Put on the Lord Jesus Christ, and make no provision for the flesh in regard to its lusts." "No provision" means to never expose yourself to sexual sin, and never provide your flesh with an opportunity to lust.

Is that how you react to sexual temptation, or do you think you can handle it? If you naively believe you can, then one way or another you will pay the consequences. You may decide you can watch a movie with naked people in it, and later find you are haunted by the images. You may choose to get more physically involved, and later discover you are not able to stop. Instead, make plans in advance to eliminate temptations.

Choose your dates wisely. Don't go out with a flirt. The only person in the Bible who flirts is a prostitute. Why would you want to go out with someone who acts like a prostitute? 1 Corinthians 15:33 says, "Do not be deceived: 'Bad company corrupts good morals.'" The bad company mentioned in that passage is a false teacher, someone with bad doctrine and an immoral lifestyle who calls himself a Christian. Avoid compromising Christians who know what the Word says but they choose to sin anyway. Their influence will poison your heart and mind.

Proceed cautiously in any relationship and get serious about sexual purity. This is war. 1 Peter 2:11 says, "Beloved, I urge you... to abstain from fleshly lusts which wage war against the soul." Don't act as if this is not a battle where bullets are flying by and bombs are constantly going off. If you get lax, you will get wounded or heartbroken.

As singles, always make sure the physical aspect of any relationship develops slowly. God's divine order of marriage is leave, cleave, and then one flesh—physical oneness should always develop last. Write down your standards at every level of relationship—develop convictions—and have your older Christian mentors hold you accountable to it. Let every area of a relationship—emotional, spiritual, social, mental and physical develop evenly. Never allow one aspect to go faster than all the others. It is always the physical aspect that wants to rush ahead of all others, distorting your understanding of the person you are trying to get to know.

Finally, pursue the things of God. 2 Timothy 2:22 says, "Now flee from youthful lusts and pursue righteousness, faith, love, and peace, with those who call on the Lord from a pure heart."

The opposite of fleeing sexual temptation is pursuing the things of God. Christians are to run after righteousness, faith, love and peace and busy themselves living out their Christianity. Then they won't have time for evil or sexual lusts.

Never forget that one of the keys to fleeing is pursuing. When you pursue Christlikeness, Bible study, serving, discipling others, witnessing, you won't have idle time to sin. Don't define your spiritual life merely by what you don't do; make sure you define it as living for Christ. Don't be like those who think they are spiritual because they "don't drink or smoke or chew or go with guys that do." Make sure the motivation for everything in life is your love for Christ.

YOUNG MARRIED WOMEN

This chapter has focused primarily on the single woman, but God gives clear direction to the married women concerning purity as well.

First, adultery is never an option. God's Word is very clear and it doesn't matter how bad your marriage is. 1 Thessalonians 4:3 says, "For this is the will of God... that you abstain from sexual immorality."

Being "in love" or attracted to someone, or even being abused by your husband, never makes adultery right. Never let your spouse doubt your fidelity. You made a vow to God and in front of many witnesses at your wedding. Honor that vow and keep your promise. God honors a wife who is faithful, even when it is difficult or seemingly impossible.

Along with adultery, keep divorce completely out of your thinking. Remove the word "divorce" from your vocabulary, because Malachi 2:16 says that God hates divorce. A sensible woman realizes that divorce is not the answer.

Second, sexual intimacy is a spiritual responsibility in marriage. 1 Corinthians 7:5 says, "Stop depriving one another, except by agreement for a time, so that you may devote yourselves to prayer, and come together again so that Satan will not tempt you because of your lack of self-control." In this passage, wives are commanded four times to have sexual relations with their husbands. God says if you neglect this area of your marriage, you're asking for trouble and you're violating the commands of Christ.

If you're married, you and your spouse have legitimate sexual needs. You are the only person who can meet those needs for your spouse, and if you don't, you are sinning. Your goal should be to fully meet the needs of your husband, so he'll think, *It's foolish to give up what I have. Why would I want anyone else besides my wife?* Proverbs 5:15-19 says, "Drink water from your own cistern and fresh water from your own well....Let your fountain be blessed, and be glad in the wife of your youth. As a loving hind and a graceful doe, let her breasts satisfy you at all times; be intoxicated always with her love."

Finally, maintain proper relationships with men other than your husband. Ephesians 5:3 says, "Sexual immorality or any impurity or greed must not even be named among you, as is proper among saints." There should not even be a hint of immorality among us. Be careful—don't send mixed signals to others, not even a hint. You need to set appropriate boundaries for dealing with men who are not your spouse. What are some appropriate boundaries?

- Never be alone with someone of the opposite sex.
- Never show personal affection to another person who is not your spouse.
- Never have an intimate discussion with another person of the opposite sex.

When you think about sexual sin, it is helpful to magnify the consequences of it in your mind, and minimize the benefits. Proverbs 6:32 says, "The one who commits adultery with a woman is lacking a heart of wisdom; he who would destroy his soul does it." Proverbs 6:26 says that adultery will cost a man all he has. And 1 Thessalonians 4:6 says that the Lord will punish those who commit immorality.

You can't get away with sexual sin. But there's incredible peace, joy and love that comes from keeping God's command to live pure. Living out purity is not something you can do on your own. You must commit to "D.O." – not "do this and don't do that," but "Depend and Obey." Depend upon the Spirit of God and step out by an act of your will to obey the Word of God.

For those of you who have already failed in this area of life, whether married or unmarried, don't forget that it's never too late to repent and ask Christ for forgiveness. The Bible says if you turn from your sin, God will wash you, cleanse you and make you whiter than snow. He will never turn you away, but will receive you and make you the beautiful woman He designed you to be. Because of God's grace through salvation, you can make today the day your purity begins.

FOR PERSONAL REFLECTION & GROUP DISCUSSION:

1. What are some of the reasons for the sexual sins in our culture today? In what ways has the church contributed to this problem?

2. What advice would you give a young teenager who wants to remain a virgin until she is married?

3. How would you respond to people who quote Jesus' words "Do not judge" when defending their practice of sexual immorality?

4. How can you plan ahead to avoid sexual temptation? Have you identified the ways you can flee if necessary?

5. How would you counsel a woman who has allowed herself to be sexually impure and is suffering from shame and regret?

8

LET THE WOMEN BE HOMEMAKERS

A GODLY WORKER AT HOME

"She watches over the ways of her household,
And does not eat the bread of idleness."

PROVERBS 31:27

Mix together a fallen culture, false teaching and some Sunday School and you will come up with some pretty confused conclusions. English teacher Richard Lederer assembled the following list of real student bloopers collected by teachers throughout the United States of eighth grade through college:

- Ancient Egypt was inhabited by mummies, and they all wrote in hydraulics. They lived in the Sarah Dessert and traveled by Camelot. Certain parts of the dessert are cultivated by irritation.
- The Bible is full of interesting caricatures. In the first book of the Bible, Guinessis, Adam and Eve were created from an apple tree. One of their children, Cain, asked, "Am I my brother's son?"

- Pharaoh forced the Hebrew slaves to make bread without straw. Moses went up on Mount Cyanide to get the ten commandments. He died before he ever reached Canada.
- David was a Hebrew king skilled at playing the liar. He fought with the Finkelsteins. Solomon, one of David's sons, had 300 wives and 700 porcupines.

"Often you are unaware that you've mixed truth with error, until God opens your eyes through His Word..."

These are funny, but in many ways you and I are also guilty of mixing modern ideas with biblical truth, resulting in incorrect conclusions. Often you are unaware that you've mixed truth with error, until God opens your eyes through His Word to show you how far you've drifted from His design. Be prepared for that to happen when you examine the issue of working moms in light of biblical truth.

Today there are about 24 million working mothers in the United States. There are also women who don't work, but are consumed with interests other than their husband, children, and home. Who does that leave to invest in the kids and manage the home?

In Titus 2:4-5 God paints a different picture of womanhood that stands in stark contrast to what we see in our world. This is the most controversial of all the qualities a young godly woman is to pursue. What is God's domestic expectation for a godly woman? "Instruct the young women in sensibility: to love their husbands, to love their children, to be sensible, pure, workers at home, kind, being subject to their own husbands, so that the Word of God will not be slandered."

This type of woman is a dynamic witness for Jesus Christ. Just a few verses later, Titus 2:11-12 tells you that because of God's grace, and because of all that Jesus Christ did for you that you could never do for yourself, you should dedicate your life to pleasing Him. You should live according to God's definition of godliness, no matter what the cost. That means women should be focused on living each of these qualities in Titus 2:4-5 by the power of the Holy Spirit. You cannot live the Christian life in your own strength.

A hotly debated quality in Paul's list is that young women should be "workers at home." In the Greek, that phrase is one word made up of a combination of two words. It literally means "home-working."

WHAT DOES IT MEAN TO BE A "WORKER AT HOME"?

The implications of this character quality cause many women in our society to hold their breath when they read it or hear it, waiting for an escape clause instead of embracing what God is calling them to do. This biblical quality will radically affect the life of everyone in your church. It affects:

- The person you marry
- The lifestyle you choose
- The marriage you maintain
- The way you parent your children
- The place you choose to live
- The career you choose

Paul's purpose in writing to Titus was to help the Cretans live according to God's design, and that is exactly what this passage will do in your life too.

WORKING HARD FOR YOUR HOME

To be a "worker at home" means that you won't be lazy, slothful, or idle. In the first century, when a Greek woman was part of a Christian family, she would enjoy a freedom that other women did not have. In the non-Christian home, the wife was treated similarly to a slave, locked in her house, and free only to do her husband's bidding.

But in Christ a woman was given freedom to minister outside of the home, to serve, care for the needy, visit the sick or prisoners, fellowship with other ladies and even to share the gospel. Because of this improved status, she also had an opportunity to turn to gossip, become idle, lazy, slothful or even immoral. This new experience created the potential for sin which had to be guarded against.

That is why "worker at home" includes the idea of working hard at home. In 1 Timothy 5:11-15 Paul says that some older widows who had lived godly, sacrificial lives were to be supported by the church so they could fulfill a unique ministry. But the younger widows were to aim their lives in a different direction. Look at the passage:

> *...Refuse to put younger widows on the list, for when they feel sensual desires in disregard of Christ, they want to get married, thus incurring condemnation, because they have set aside their previous pledge. And at the same time they also learn to be idle, as they go around from house to house. And not merely idle, but also gossips and busybodies, talking about things not proper to mention. Therefore, I want younger widows to get married, bear children, keep house, and give the enemy no opportunity for reviling; for some have already turned aside after Satan.*

Why is it so important for the older women to train younger women to become hard workers at home? Paul says that if they don't, the younger women may learn to be idle. The Greek word for "idle" is used elsewhere to describe someone who is unemployed and careless, with nothing to do. We know this was a problem on Crete because in Titus 1:12 Paul says the description of Cretans as lazy gluttons is accurate. "Lazy" in Titus 1:12 is the same word as "idle" in 1 Timothy 5:13, and the consequences for this behavior are very serious. Paul says in 1 Timothy 5:13 that idleness leads to sins of the mouth, like gossip. Proverbs 19:15 says, "Laziness casts into a deep sleep, and a slack-handed soul will suffer hunger." Proverbs 24:33-34 says, "'A little sleep, a little slumber, a little folding of the hands to rest,' then your poverty will come as a robber and your want like an armed man."

In contrast, the godly woman isn't lazy, careless or negligent, but is willing to work hard. This is how Proverbs 31:27 describes her: "She watches over the ways of her household, and does not eat the bread of idleness."

"The character of a godly woman is that of a hard worker."

Godliness is not merely the externals of Christianity, like carrying a Bible and attending church. The character of a godly woman is that of a hard worker. When Paul tells Titus that women are to be workers at home, the Greek word for "work" means hard labor and the accomplishment of difficult tasks.

What does a homemaker do all day? The following list is adapted from an article by Linda Weber in *Focus on the Family* magazine (April 1994). A homemaker is the...

- baby feeder, changer, bather, burper, hugger and listener to fussing and thousands of questions
- picker-upper of food and debris cast on the floor
- linguistic expert for two-year-old dialects
- listener to the husband and children about their day, needs, concerns, aspirations

- teacher of everything from how to chew food to how to drive a car
- laundry maintenance engineer and ironer of wrinkles
- assistant on school projects
- censor of TV, movies and books
- reader of thousands of children's books
- planner and hostess of children's birthday parties, dinner parties and holidays
- organizer of the kitchen, the living room, the bathrooms, the chores, the routine, the division of labor
- executioner of ants, roaches, wasps and other pests
- resident historian in charge of photo albums, baby books and school record books
- resident correspondent to relatives and old family friends
- keeper and locator of all valuable documents
- appointment desk for the family's visits to the doctor, dentist, orthodontist, barber and the mechanic
- cleaner of the oven, the drawers, the closets, the garage, the curtains, the windows and even the walls
- interior decorator
- emergency medical technician and ambulance driver
- hubby's best friend, confidant and romantic focus

God calls young women to be workers at home—therefore, all her chores are spiritual work to glorify Him. Understand, we're encouraged to work hard because God does. Philippians 2:13 says, "For it is God who is at work in you, both to will and to work for His good pleasure." And Jesus says in John 5:17, "My Father is working until now, and I Myself am working." Our God is a working God—He is active in and through all circumstances to bring about His will. Because He is a working God, all who desire to be godly, or God-like, will work hard too.

Another reason we must learn to work hard is because hard work is an important part of God's purpose for us. Today people plan and scheme how they can get out of work, but we need to realize that our work has been pre-planned for us. Ephesians 2:10 says, "For we are His workmanship, created in Christ Jesus for good works, which God prepared beforehand so that we would walk in them."

Remember that God gave Adam work before the fall. What God set in place before the fall was good, therefore work is good. It is part of our created purpose. Work is meant to be a joy and blessing.

"We learn to work hard by example...and mothers train their daughters. That's why the older women are to train the younger women to be workers at home."

We learn to work hard by example. Fathers train their sons and mothers train their daughters. That's why the older women are to train the younger women to be workers at home. The ability to work hard is something that is learned through mentoring and modeling.

Hard work is a character quality that God rewards with the blessings of food and shelter, satisfaction of a job well done, being a strong witness and even sleeping well at night. All faithful believers should learn to work hard and God designed married women to work hard in the home.

COMMITING TO THE PRIORITY OF THE HOME

Paul makes a dramatic statement in 1 Timothy 5:14: "I want younger widows to get married, bear children, keep house, and give the enemy no opportunity for reviling." God's design for younger women is to get married, have kids and "keep house."

The Greek word for "keep house" is a very strong word. It comes from two words, "house" and "master." The Greek word for "master" is despotes and is where we get the English word "despot." So 1 Timothy 5:14 is saying that young married women should be managers and masters of the home—they should rule or run the household. They are the home despots.

The role of a woman, by God's design, includes a strong commitment to the priority and management of the home. She is the master of the home who brings order because she follows the God of order (1 Corinthians 14:33).

The Bible does not condone the woman who spends her days at home watching soap operas, posting on social media, following Christian bloggers, shopping endlessly online or other unfruitful activities. She should be working hard to make her home reflect the orderliness that is part of God's character. Unlike the harlot described in Proverbs 7:11 ("Her feet do not dwell at home"), the godly woman is at home, overseeing her household for the spiritual benefit of her family and for God's glory.

The world pictures the homemaker as a prisoner who is overworked, confined, bored, frustrated, out of her mind and missing out on the good life. God views the role of a wife as the master of the home who lives out her commitment in freedom, contentment, peace and joy. She manages the affairs of her home so that her husband and children are blessed in countless ways (Proverbs 31:10-31).

A HOME REFLECTS A WOMAN'S CHARACTER

In Proverbs 14:1, God tells us something about our houses. "The wise woman builds her house, but the woman of folly tears it down with her own hands. Notice the Proverb says that what happens in the home is a reflection of the character of its occupants. So for a woman, her home is an extension of her character. A person's character can be revealed in several ways. A crisis can help you see a person's grit; a bank statement can tell you about someone's heart; a calendar can show you a woman's priorities and the home will indicate a wife's character, values and so much more.

How would you describe your home, your apartment or even your room? Is it comfortable or stiff, economical or extravagant, welcoming or restricting, formal or casual, happy or depressing, orderly or chaotic, hospitable or hostile? When you describe a home, you are also, to some degree, describing the woman who manages that home.

The key to understanding "workers at home" is not her decorative ability, nice furniture or other externals, but her heart. Some women work at home, but have the wrong heart. Others may work outside the home, but their heart's desire is with their family at home. Is your heart committed to your family and home first? My goal is not to upset anyone or make you feel pressure or guilt. My goal is simply to teach what the Bible says and try to work through some of the implications of what God desires for you.

ACCEPTING THE HEART OF GOD FOR A WOMAN IN THE HOME

Let's read Titus 2:4-5 again and look for the qualities that are important to God: "Instruct the young women in sensibility: to love their husbands, to love their children, to be sensible, pure, workers at home, kind, being subject to their own husbands, so that the Word of God will not be slandered." And 1 Timothy 5:14: "Therefore, I want younger widows to get married, bear children, keep house, and give the enemy no opportunity for reviling."

As I've studied the Word and taught on this issue, my heart has been filled with deep concern for single moms with kids, families struggling to make ends meet, newly married women, my friends at church who want to follow the Bible and particularly single young women. I want you to know that my desire is to speak the truth in love about this difficult issue. And I realize that some of what I say will run counter to our culture, and even to what is taught in the vast majority of churches in America.

The phrase "workers at home" is from the Greek words oikos (home) and ergon (work). But ergon (work) does not usually refer to labor in general. It often refers to a particular job or employment. It is the word Jesus used when He said, "My food is to do the will of Him who sent Me and to finish His work" (John 4:34). Our Lord focused His entire life on fulfilling God's will—God's work.

"...a wife is to focus her life's work on the home. God has designed the family to be her main sphere of influence, her main place of responsibility."

In a similar fashion, a wife is to focus her life's work on the home. God has designed the family to be her main sphere of influence, her main place of responsibility. It doesn't mean she must spend 24 hours a day there. The woman in Proverbs 31, for example, left her home to buy a field or when she needed supplies. But those trips away from the home benefited her family. She poured her life into her family. She woke up early and went to bed late for the sake of those in her home.

Notice Paul didn't make any attempt to elaborate on what he meant by "workers at home." That's because his readers were completely familiar with the term. First century writings tell us what life was like for a woman in Paul's day. She was expected to grind the flour, bake the bread, launder the clothes by hand, cook the meals over a fire, nurse and care for her children, make the beds, keep the house clean, spin the wool, prepare the children for school and get them there. While many women also worked with their husbands in the field or in a trade, it was the husband's responsibility to provide food, clothing, and housing.

A wife could work at crafts or horticulture in the home and sell the fruits of her labor. Profits from her efforts could be used to supplement her husband's income or provide her with some spending money for the household. And in addition to the household chores, wives were responsible for hospitality, for the care of guests and for charitable work. In other words, she was to care for the needs of her husband, home, children, guests, strangers, the poor and the needy. Wives who did so were respected in the community.

Today, we have many conveniences that ancient people did not have. We don't have to grind our own grain, spin wool to make fabric or go to a river to wash clothes. That means "workers at home" have more time, but they need to be careful to use that time well. More time does not change the godly woman's priorities. There may be opportunities to do more things that will benefit the home and be helpful to others. There may even be time for enterprising and entrepreneurial opportunities like those described in the life of the Proverbs 31 woman. She worked to bring in some extra income. But the home should remain the priority.

The Bible says that God's heart, God's design and God's plan is for women to be workers at home. The world will do anything it can to disrupt and distort God's perfect design. Ask yourself this question: Is it God's will for young Christian mothers to be workers at home? Yes, the Bible is clear. So is it God's will for young Christian mothers to work outside the home? Very rarely.

WHY WORK AT HOME?

I will address some exceptions to this and explain why the answer to the second question is, 'very rarely'. I will further provide application to the single woman and how she is to apply this principle.

SCRIPTURAL ISSUES

I believe that the command to be "workers at home" is a biblical absolute, not an outdated cultural tradition or personal opinion. Being a worker at home is not a gray area. A gray area is an issue that the Scripture does not directly address, like playing cards or using make-up. The Bible says nothing directly about these issues, so you have to use the general principles of God's Word to decide what you should or should not do in any given situation. However, "workers at home" is clearly addressed in several Scripture passages (Titus 2:4-5, 1Timothy 5:14, Proverbs 31).

There is no confusion about what God had in mind when He said women should be workers at home and keep house. Almost all the examples of godly women in both the Old and New Testaments had a clear focus toward the home. There is no clear command or direction in the Bible for a woman to do anything other than work in and through her home. Modern-day professing Christians love to use the cultural excuse on these verses, which is really nothing less than asking, "Is that really what God intended?"

"Workers at home" clearly sets a direction toward the home, not away from it. This is another reason why the proper answer to the question, "Should a young Christian mother work outside the home?" is "very rarely," rather than "maybe" or "it depends." The answer is "very rarely" because working in the home is God's stated will for women. So when you feel like doing something contrary to that direction, you should fight it. The true Christian's desire is to move toward God's will, not away from God's will. And Scripture teaches us God's will.

Consider this similar issue: Does God want you to go to church each week? Of course He does. Hebrews 10:25 says we should not be "forsaking our own assembling together, as is the habit of some, but encouraging one another; and all the more as you see the day drawing near." So if you can't go to church because of your work schedule, you will be praying to change jobs or change your schedule. All true Christians want to be obedient to God's clear commands instead of trying to find a way around it.

God wants women to be workers at home, so our response should be the same. We should do everything we can to live in conformity to God's plan as outlined in His Word—not legalistically, but from a heart that wants to obey the Savior who did everything for us.

Making "workers at home" optional would mean that the rest of the qualities in Titus 2:4-5 are optional too. If you somehow think you can come to the conclusion that being a worker at home is an option for your family, then look at the context of this passage. If "workers at home" is optional, then it must also be optional for women to love their husbands, love their children, be sensible and pure, be kind, and live in subjection to their husbands. You can't isolate one item on the list, especially the one in the middle and call it optional, then view the rest of the qualities as requirements. The heart of a godly woman will never pick and choose which truths of Scripture she will follow.

ADDITIONAL ISSUES

The first issue is the managing of priorities. A sensible young woman knows her priorities. Her main priority is to meet the needs of her family—love her husband and children. She shows her love for her husband and children by making the home a place of peace and rest.

A second priority for young mothers is the training of their children. 1 Timothy 2:15 says that women "will be saved through the bearing of children, if they continue in faith and love and sanctification with self-restraint." This verse teaches that a wife will find her greatest usefulness in raising children. The Greek word for "bearing of children" means more than merely giving birth to children—it also encompasses the idea of raising children. This verse teaches that instilling values in children is an important part of a mother's role. Proverbs 6:20 also teaches that mothers play a crucial role in teaching children the truths of Scripture. "My son, observe the commandment of your father and do not abandon the law of your mother."

The third priority is ministering to the needs of the poor and underprivileged. "She extends her hand to the poor; and she stretches out her hands to the needy (Proverbs 31:20)."

A wife who fulfills those three priorities will be very busy. If she still has time left over, she would then be free to pursue enterprising or creative activities outside the home. Those who are most free to do these things are women with no children at home. Even these women should be sure they're fulfilling their responsibilities at home before they go into the workplace.

The Bible does not explicitly state that women, even those with small children, cannot work outside the home. However, the Bible does say that a woman's role is to care for the home. The biggest issue that a working mom will face is time. Any activity outside the home that keeps her from fulfilling her role in the home will not be best for her or her family.

The second major issue with young Christian mothers working outside the home is the problem of authority. Ephesians 5:22 says, "Wives, be subject to your own husbands, as to the Lord" and 1 Peter 3:1 says, "You wives, be subject to your own husbands." When women work outside the home, they are now also in submission to an employer, and this can create difficult situations for both the husband and wife. What happens, for example, when the husband wants her to come home on time, but the boss wants her to work late?

Conflict between various authorities can happen to anyone. As a pastor I've seen where the dangers are greater in this particular situation, because the challenges of an employer-employee relationship and a couple still learning how to make marriage work are two of the hardest to navigate. The pressure and demands of a job while maintaining the priorities of the home can build up unhealthy tensions in a marriage.

A third issue is the problem of motive. The most common

reason both a husband and wife work outside the home is because they desire more income to maintain the lifestyle they want. Often it is not based on need, but greed.

This is an issue of the heart. The difference between having enough to live on and wanting more to support a lifestyle is huge—one motive is godly and the other is worldly. One motive pursues God's priorities out of a love for Him and the other pursues a love for the things of the world. Many couples today make poor financial choices, pursuing material comforts instead of sacrificing and saving over time. It's an issue of motive that only God, you and your spouse can identify and determine. I encourage you to honestly examine it with an open heart. Pray along with the Psalmist, "Search me, O God, and know my heart...and see if there be any hurtful way in me" (Psalm 139:23-24).

The Bible does not explicitly state that women, even those with small children, cannot work outside the home. But it seems very clear that those who are free to work outside the home are single women, married women with no children and mothers with young adult children. What God desires is a heart that is genuinely and primarily focused on making the home a place where He is glorified and His purposes are accomplished.

UNIQUE ISSUES

What about the young single mother? First, according to the Bible, you should pursue reconciliation with your spouse if you were divorced unbiblically (1 Corinthians 7:10-11). If that's not possible, then God's priority for you is to remarry (1 Timothy 5:14). You might say, "I would like to do that, but have you seen what the dating field looks like out there?" Never compromise God's standard for marriage. Don't date men who are unbelievers or pretend believers or marginal believers. Wait for someone who will lead your family biblically—don't put your children at risk by marrying unwisely.

While you wait on God to bring another husband into your life, do everything you can to live close to the church body. Become involved, even though it's hard to do as a single parent. Pray that God will open up opportunities for close friends within the church to be an extension of your own family.

What about the young widow? 1 Timothy 5:11-13 warns that younger widows can be easily tempted into sensuality, idleness, and gossip. So God says it is better for those younger widows to remarry. Verse 14 says, "Therefore, I want younger widows to get married, bear children, keep house, and give the enemy no opportunity for reviling."

The heart of the issue is still God's priority of home and family for women. For young widows, remarriage is the place where growth in godliness will occur. But again, don't compromise God's standard for marriage—be prudent, not desperate to remarry. 1 Corinthians 7:39 says, "A wife is bound as long as her husband lives; but if her husband has fallen asleep, she is free to be married to whom she wishes, only in the Lord."

The death of a spouse is extremely painful, yet brought about by a loving God. Trust God's timing; His timing will be perfect in leading you into marriage again, if your heart stays open to the priority of home and family. Don't turn your eyes to the world for happiness or fulfillment. If you pursue an independent lifestyle, it will be difficult for you to come under the headship of a husband once again.

What about the young wife whose husband wants her to work outside the home? Many women face this dilemma, in which a tension arises between two biblical principles: God's plan for wives to be "workers at home" (1 Timothy 5:14; Titus 2:4-5) and His command to submit to their husbands (Ephesians 5:22). Here are some thoughts for women who find themselves in this situation:

- First, begin praying that God would sovereignly work in your husband's heart.
- Then, making sure you have the right motives—love for your husband and family and love for God—share your

convictions with your husband. Let him know that obedience to God is what matters most to you. Maybe you can find a creative way to work and still be at home, or limit your time away from home.

- If your husband claims to be a Christian, and refuses to grant your request, then you should involve the counsel of your church elders or leaders. During the time you seek counsel, however, continue to obey your husband by working outside of the home.
- If efforts fail to persuade your husband that this is God's will, then submit to him and continue praying and fasting that he will follow God's design for your marriage.

1 Peter 3:1-2 says that wives should demonstrate their love for God by submitting to the leadership of their husbands, even if their husbands "are disobedient to the Word." By working outside the home in submission to her husband, a wife can take comfort knowing that God is sovereign. God knows her circumstances and is able to honor her faithfulness by working in her husband's heart. And even if he does not change, God says that "if you should suffer for the sake of righteousness, you are blessed" (1 Peter 3:14).

HOW TO MAKE A DECISION ABOUT WORKING

Here are some questions to consider about working outside the home:

- Will it remove or hinder you from your obligations in the home?
- Will it make it difficult to submit to your husband's authority?
- What is your motive? Will your family become dependent upon your income?
- Will this job put you in any type of compromising position?

Some women have no choice but to work outside the home. If the reason is to get out of debt—then yes, maybe you need to work. If it's to do ministry—well, perhaps. But if your motive is to raise your standard of living or gratify your personal need for significance, then probably not.

A woman's greatest impact for the kingdom of God will be her influence in the lives of her children. That's why Paul said to Timothy that motherhood would be her "salvation" (1 Timothy 2:15). She will impact the kingdom from the bottom up, rather than from the top down.

THOUGHTS FOR YOUNG SINGLE WOMEN

In today's culture, single Christian women live in a state of tension, especially after they graduate from high school. They are still under their father's authority, yet they are not under a husband's authority, so what should they do?

If you are in this category, you should obviously do everything you can to live to the glory of God, imitating Christ through obedience to the Word of God by the power of the Holy Spirit. If you are in school, make sure you are going there for the right reasons—not for self or pride, but so you can grow to be more like Christ, evangelize the lost, equip Christians and develop other skills necessary to live for God's glory in any situation. Don't pursue a career for money or lifestyle but to worship the Lord, serve others and learn the character of Christ. Don't even minister in the church for yourself, but to please God and build the body of Christ.

Young Christian women must live responsibly and faithfully. Live by faith and prepare now for the role of wife, mother and homemaker—it's a huge job. Yes, it is mocked by the world, but nothing is more demanding nor rewarding.

Watch and practice domestic skills. Learn the skills of proper nutrition, budgeting, banking, Bible study, prayer, etc. Learn a balance between present ministry (church, school, career, missions) and future ministry (marriage, family, and home). Learn to maintain a proper relationship with your parents.

Prepare now to work at home. Learn to live in an orderly manner—can you see the floor of your room? If you can't organize your room, how will you manage an entire house? Learn the skills needed for motherhood now. Don't end up being the wife who only knows how to burn water. Learn how to shop, cook, prepare, clean, plan meals and do it all inexpensively.

If you were raised by a godly mother, then learn from her, and if not her, then godly older women. This is the only practice you'll get. Work on becoming the kind of woman described in Proverbs 31:27-30 which says, "She watches over the ways of her household, and does not eat the bread of idleness. Her children rise up and bless her; as for her husband, he also praises her, saying: 'Many daughters have done excellently, but you have gone above them all.' Charm is deceitful and beauty is vain, but a woman who fears Yahweh, she shall be praised."

As we recognize that our culture has little tolerance for God's Word and what it calls women to do and be, we realize anyone who holds to the Scripture will be maligned. Those who believe what the Bible instructs and seek to obey His truth will be ridiculed, thought to be crazy and old-fashioned. We can expect that our lifestyle will not reflect the world, and it shouldn't.

If you find the principles from this chapter difficult to accept, can I encourage you to look hard at what the Bible has to say about this? Our culture has moved further and further away from God's design. It may cost you a serious relationship or your career aspirations to move back to His original design. Yet, I truly believe it will be best for you in the end. Wrestling through this issue will be worth it, as you seek God's will in God's Word and trust Him to break down all the barriers that stand in the way of His perfect plan for you.

FOR PERSONAL REFLECTION & GROUP DISCUSSION:

1. What arguments have you heard for and against women working outside the home? Which do you find most convincing?

2. How have you personally seen God use homemakers to bless others and expand His kingdom in the world?

3. How would you describe the character of the home you live in? Would you say it represents the character of a godly woman?

4. Examine your motives for working and/or going to school. Are these goals leading you into marriage or are they creating barriers?

5. What are several ways a single woman can begin to prepare for the future role of homemaker?

9

LET THE WOMEN BE KIND

A GODLY WOMAN IS KIND

"Instead, be kind to one another, tender-hearted, graciously forgiving each other, just as God in Christ also has graciously forgiven you."

EPHESIANS 4:32

Little Chad was a shy, quiet young boy. One day he came home from school and told his mom he wanted to make a Valentine for each person in class. His mom's heart sank thinking, I wish he wouldn't do that. She had watched the children when they walked home from school hanging onto each other, talking and laughing. Chad always walked behind them and was never included. Nevertheless, she decided to go along with her son's idea, and she purchased the paper, glue and crayons he needed to make the Valentines.

For three whole weeks, night after night, Chad painstakingly made 35 Valentines. Valentine's Day dawned, and Chad was overflowing with excitement! He carefully stacked the Valentines, put them in a bag, and bolted out the door for school.

His mom decided to bake his favorite cookies with a cool glass of milk because it would ease his pain. It hurt her to think about how her son wouldn't get many Valentines, maybe none.

That afternoon she had the snack on the table waiting for him. She looked out the window when she heard the children coming. Sure enough, they were laughing and having the best time. Again, Chad was bringing up the rear, though he seemed to be walking a little faster than usual. She noticed his arms were empty, and fully expected him to burst into tears as soon as he came inside.

When the door opened, she choked back her tears and said, "I made your favorite cookies." But Chad hardly heard her words. He marched right on by, his face aglow. All he said was, "Not a one … not a one." His mother's heart sank. But then he added, "I didn't forget one person!"

Little Chad's unselfish act of giving touches our hearts because it reminds us of who Christ is and who we should be. Those who follow Christ as their Master are to be kind.

"[Kindness] is one of the essential character qualities of the young woman who is in pursuit of glorifying God."

THE IMPORTANCE OF KINDNESS

Kindness should be a quality that people associate with Christians. We find kindness listed among the attributes for godly women in Titus 2:4-5. It is one of the essential character qualities of the young woman who is in pursuit of glorifying God.

Would your circle of friends consider you a kind person? Titus 2:4-5 says, "Instruct the young women in sensibility: to love their husbands, to love their children, to be sensible, pure, workers at home, kind, being subject to their own husbands, so that the Word of God will not be slandered."

The word "kind" in the Greek text is agathos. It is translated "good" or "kind" in most verses in which it is found. But when agathos is used to describe the character or activity of people, it takes on a more specific meaning. It means they are not only good or kind but also fit, capable and useful. In other words, a kind person is one who is capable of representing Christ.

When agathos is used to describe someone's activity, the word speaks of a commitment to excellence. It describes a person who causes others to benefit from her deeds of kindness. The kind person acts out of goodness and generosity for the benefit of others. Like Christ, this person manifests a genuine spirit of compassion, with wisdom and discernment.

Christlike kindness is not shown to make the giver the focal point, but rather to build up and encourage others. Biblical kindness is not a way to appear religious, but instead to share Christ and display His character. God wants Christians to be intentionally kind in order to show people what Jesus is like.

Paul says that women are to seek opportunities to be kind. This was a problem for the saints on Crete. Not only did Cretans struggle with being lazy, they didn't think it necessary to display how God changed their lives. They didn't think they had to live any differently from the world, but only had to believe in Jesus.

So Paul exhorts them six times in just three chapters to be doers of good deeds.

- Titus 1:16: They profess to know God, but by their works they deny Him, being detestable and disobedient and unfit for any good work.
- Titus 2:7a: In all things show yourself to be a model of good works.
- Titus 2:14: [Christ] gave Himself for us that He might redeem us from all lawlessness, and purify for Himself a

people for His own possession, zealous for good works.
- Titus 3:1: Remind them…to be ready for every good work.
- Titus 3:8b: Those who have believed God will be intent to lead in good works. These things are good and profitable for men.
- Titus 3:14: Our people must also learn to lead in good works to meet pressing needs, so that they will not be unfruitful.

Paul tells Titus to encourage and exhort the Cretans to engage in good works. What was needed on Crete were thinking women who loved their husbands and children, lived morally pure lives, had a commitment to the home and were socially kind. Their homes were to be places seasoned with kindness in word and deed. Their character would overflow to a society desperately in need of Christ. The fruit of these women's ministries was not only resulting in people hearing the gospel, but in the lost actually seeing Christ in their kindness. They not only wanted their husbands, children, church and friends to become more like Christ; they also wanted their neighbors, unsaved family and others to know Christ.

Older women should train younger women to be kind. When your church is filled with women who practice kindness, the lost will be drawn to Jesus and God will be glorified. You'll only exhibit this kindness by the power of the Holy Spirit working in you.

Once a frustrated seminary student was laboring to finish his thesis, which was due the next day. At 11:00 p.m. with only three pages of his 100-page thesis typed, he knew it was impossible to finish by the deadline. The student called his seminary professor James Rosscup, waking him and asking for an extension. Dr. Rosscup thought for a moment and responded, "No, but I'll come over and type it for you."

The flustered student mumbled "Oh, you don't have to do that" and hung up. Three minutes later his phone rang with Dr. Rosscup saying, "I'm dressed and ready. I'll be over in a few minutes to type." And that's what he did! Just like Jesus Christ, Dr. Rosscup's sacrifice demonstrated true kindness.

You may ask, "How can I learn to be kind like that?" One helpful way is to remember the acrostic K-I-N-D.

- K: Knowing God's Heart
- I: Initiating Sacrificial Good Deeds
- N: Nurturing the Needy
- D: Developing Christlike Discernment.

KNOWING GOD'S HEART

Look with me at some key passages that describe God's heart of kindness. Romans 2:4 exposes religious people who accuse others of sin while excusing their own: "Or do you think lightly of the riches of His kindness and forbearance and patience, not knowing that the kindness of God leads you to repentance?"

Just because your life is going well doesn't mean you are right with God. He is patient and has been very kind to you. The good things in your life should not be taken for granted, but should produce praise and thanksgiving. He provides good things so you will only depend on Him.

God is a kind God. He is even good to His enemies. But eventually God's patience will cease and so will His kindness. Romans 2 says on a future day, God will judge with righteous justice and holy wrath (v. 5). But God is a kind God—He is kind to all people, even those who judge others wrongly and excuse their own sin.

When you know God's heart, you'll be kind too. In fact, kindness is so important to God that He repeatedly commands you and me to be kind. In Colossians 3:12-13, Paul says, "As the elect of God, holy and beloved, put on a heart of compassion, kindness, humility, gentleness, and patience; bearing with one another, and graciously forgiving each other, whoever has a complaint against anyone, just as the Lord graciously forgave you, so also should you."

We are commanded to "put on" kindness like a shirt or blouse, an article of clothing that will be noticed. Kindness is one of the most attractive garments in the Christian's wardrobe. We're not merely to be kind when we feel like it or happen to think about it. The true Christian works at kindness out of obedience to Christ.

A MATTER OF OBEDIENCE

When a sergeant says to a private, "Go dig a ditch," the private doesn't say, "OK, when I feel like it." He doesn't even say, "I think that's a good idea." The private has no choice. He obeys, "Yes, sir!" Christian kindness is an act of obedience, it is not optional for the woman who loves Jesus Christ.

We can only be kind by choosing to live life God's way instead of ours. Kindness is a fruit of the Spirit (Galatians 5:22). When you become a Christian, the Holy Spirit comes to live in you, and He will direct you to be kind toward others.

True kindness is not expressed naturally in people apart from God. It doesn't start with your feelings. Kindness is the result of a dependent choice of your will. You won't find biblical kindness when you wake up in the morning and look in the mirror. Don't expect a rush of emotion moving you to be kind. You will become truly kind only as you yield to the Holy Spirit, moment by moment.

"Kindness produced by the Holy Spirit is not limited to friends, family or those we know at church. True kindness is expressed even to enemies."

EVEN TO ENEMIES

Kindness produced by the Holy Spirit is not limited to friends, family or those we know at church. True kindness is expressed even to enemies.

In 2 Timothy 2:24-26, Paul exhorts Timothy to be kind even to the enemies of Christ, so that they might see the true Christ and repent. Paul says, "The Lord's slave must not be quarrelsome, but be kind to all, able to teach, patient when wronged, with gentleness correcting those who are in opposition, if perhaps God may give them repentance leading to the full knowledge of the truth, and they may come to their senses and escape from the snare of the devil, having been held captive by him to do his will." We're to be kind to all, even those who might do us harm, so they would turn to Christ.

In Titus 3:4-5, we learn that such kindness is rooted in the character of God: "When the kindness and affection of God our Savior appeared, He saved us, not by works which we did in righteousness, but according to His mercy, through the washing of regeneration and renewing by the Holy Spirit." Since God is so kind, we are to be kind too.

"It was the kindness of God that sent Christ to save us. When Christians display that same type of kindness, it reveals Christ to those who desperately need Him."

It was the kindness of God that sent Christ to save us. When Christians display that same type of kindness, it reveals Christ to those who desperately need Him. Do you know and live out the kindness of God? Kindness will be increasingly evident in a young woman who desires to be obedient to the Father, seeks to model Christ and depends on the Holy Spirit.

INITIATING SACRIFICIAL GOOD DEEDS

The bumper sticker, "Practice random acts of kindness," is a nice sentiment. True biblical kindness is shown when we initiate sacrificial good deeds to meet the real needs of another. You might say, "Lots of people do good deeds." That's right, but true Christian kindness is very different from the kindness of the world.

RADICAL

Luke 6:27-31 states:

> *I say to you who hear, love your enemies, do good to those who hate you, bless those who curse you, pray for those who disparage you. Whoever hits you on the cheek, offer him the other also; and whoever takes away your garment, do not withhold your tunic from him either. Give to everyone who asks of you, and whoever takes away what is yours, do not demand it back. And treat others the same way you want them to treat you.*

The Golden Rule is God's standard for kindness, but Jesus takes it a step further in verses 32-34:

> *And if you love those who love you, what credit is that to you? For even sinners love those who love them. And if you do good to those who do good to you, what credit is that to you? For even sinners do the same. And if you lend to those from whom you expect to receive, what credit is that to you? Even sinners lend to sinners in order to receive back the same amount.*

This Christlike kindness is not natural and not normal. True kindness is not necessarily fun, easy or convenient. It is supernatural and contrary to everything our society tells you to do toward unloving, rotten, selfish people. The world tells you to treat them like trash. God tells you to treat them with love, the same way Christ treats his enemies.

Verses 35-36 say, "Love your enemies, and do good, and lend, expecting nothing in return; and your reward will be great, and you will be sons of the Most High; for He Himself is kind to the ungrateful and evil. Be merciful, just as your Father is merciful."

What's our normal response to ungrateful or unloving people? We ignore them or retaliate and give them some of the same. God says the true test of kindness is not when people are nice, but when they're rotten to us. If you're kind when people are cruel, then you are truly kind.

Unless you've shown kindness in hostile situations, you don't really know true Christian kindness. Kindness is not only reserved for friends, family, other Christians, or for those who smile at you and act nice. It's also for when people hate and reject you. When you respond in kindness is when you are like Christ.

PRACTICAL

Acts 9:36-39 teaches us that Christian kindness means initiating sacrificial good deeds even when it's a person who never can repay you. This passage in Acts shows the heart of the early church:

> *Now in Joppa there was a disciple named Tabitha (which translated is called Dorcas). This woman was full of good works and charity which she continually did. And it happened at that time that she fell sick and died; and when they had washed her body, they laid it in an upper room. Now since Lydda was near Joppa, the disciples, having heard that Peter was there, sent two men to him, pleading with him, "Do not delay in coming to us." So Peter arose and went with them. When he arrived, they brought him into the upper*

room; and all the widows stood beside him, crying and showing all the tunics and garments that Dorcas used to make while she was with them.

Then Peter raised her from the dead. Notice in verse 36 how Dorcus was known for her deeds of kindness. This was the habit of her life, the pattern of her character. Verse 39 says she made tunics and garments for the widows. Dorcus was a kind and generous woman who put her sewing skills to use and donated clothing to those who were less fortunate. Showing kindness means using your talents, time and treasure to meet the needs of others.

"Showing kindness means using your talents, time and treasure to meet the needs of others."

INTENTIONAL

Initiating good deeds is radical, practical and intentional. Biblical kindness is knowing God's heart and initiating random deeds of kindness, but it also should have a particular focus.

1 Thessalonians 5:15 says, "See that no one repays another with evil for evil, but always seek after that which is good for one another and for all people." Rather than allowing revenge or hostility to reign in your heart, you should eagerly pursue what is kind toward others. The Bible not only expects Christians to be kind, but presses us to purposely look for opportunities to do kind deeds. A few practical ways to do this are:

- loving new visitors at church, answering any questions and taking them to lunch
- assisting the unfortunate, widows or orphans

- helping a distressed traveler
- sharing an encouraging word
- sending a thoughtful gift, writing a note of appreciation
- assisting the elderly, helping with chores or just visiting them.

NURTURING THE NEEDY

Godly women have a heart to minister to the needy, the poor and the hurting. This describes the Proverbs 31 woman. Verse 20 reads, "She extends her hand to the poor, and she stretches out her hands to the needy." "Poor" means afflicted, humble, lowly and oppressed. The godly woman has so much love to give that it doesn't stop with her family. Her hands are continually outstretched to anyone in need. And she doesn't merely go to the downtown mission to help the needy. She looks down the street in her neighborhood or down the row where she is sitting at church.

Showing kind deeds to the needy is so important to the Lord that He created an office in the church to make sure it happens—the office of deacon. One of the functions of deacons is to minister to the needy. Look at Acts 6:1-3:

> *Now in those days, while the disciples were multiplying in number, there was grumbling from the Hellenists against the Hebrews, because their widows were being overlooked in the daily serving of food. So the twelve summoned the congregation of the disciples and said, "It is not pleasing to God for us to neglect the Word of God in order to serve tables. Therefore, brothers, select from among you seven men of good reputation, full of the Spirit and of wisdom, whom we may put in charge of this need.*

The widows were being overlooked, so instead of turning the

attention of the apostles to that need and thereby neglecting their ministries of teaching and prayer, God established the office of deacon. The deacons were qualified Christians who oversaw the care of the needy in the church. As the church grew and spread, the eldership was always established first in new local congregations. But as those churches grew, the responsibility to care for the needy also grew, and then deacons would be appointed.

James 1:27 reveals God's heart toward the needy, "Pure and undefiled religion before our God and Father is this: to visit orphans and widows in their affliction, and to keep oneself unstained by the world." If you have God's heart, then you will be like these individuals who are described in Scripture.

- Dorcus, who showed her concern for the needy by making garments for them
- Joseph of Arimathea, who provided Jesus with a tomb for his burial (Luke 23:50-53)
- Barnabas, who sold a tract of land and gave it unconditionally to the apostles for the needs of the early church (Acts 4:36-37).

DEVELOPING CHRISTLIKE DISCERNMENT

Kindness is not meant to be blind. Initiating good deeds and nurturing the needy must also embrace Christlike discernment. Being kind should never be separated from the truth of God's Word or godly wisdom. In Titus 2:5, kindness is mentioned right next to sensibility. The God of love, mercy, and grace is also the God of holiness, justice and wrath. The kind woman of God must also be a woman of truth and justice.

For Christians there are three key principles to consider. First, don't violate the truth of God's Word. If kindness is ever expressed contrary to the Scriptures, it is not the kindness of God. In the early church there were phony Christians who thought everyone owed them a living. Like many in society, they embraced the role of victim. Any kindness to them fed their lazy selfishness. God wisely says in 2 Thessalonians 3:10, "If anyone is not willing to work, neither let him eat." Having discernment will prevent acts of kindness from being abused.

The second principle is not to hinder the growth of Christians. You cannot spare Christians from dealing with the consequences of their sin. You can't prevent every trial they may face. Galatians 6:7 reminds us, "Do not be deceived, God is not mocked, for whatever a man sows, this he will also reap."

If a Christian steals something, you're not being kind by replacing it yourself. The one who stole should bring it back or pay for it and deal with the consequences. Don't hinder their growth by your kindness. Remember, God's discipline is one way for Christians to repent and grow.

A third principle is to discern when there is a real need and take action. Don't merely say kind things, do kind things. James 2:14-17 says, "What use is it, my brothers, if someone says he has faith but he has no works? Can that faith save him? If a brother or sister is without clothing and in need of daily food, and one of you says to them, 'Go in peace, be warmed and be filled,' and yet you do not give them what is necessary for their body, what use is that? Even so faith, if it has no works, is dead by itself."

WITH NON-CHRISTIANS

Romans 2:4 says that the kindness of God can lead them to repentance. Titus 3:4-5 says that the kindness of God saved us. Titus 2:5 says to be kind so that the Word of God may not be slandered. The goal of God's kindness is to bring non-Christians to repentance. And the goal of your kindness to the lost should be the same, to build bridges for the gospel.

A discerning Christian tries not to facilitate the sin of others through their acts of kindness. For example, instead of giving money to the homeless, give food, clothing or fast-food gift cards. Consider sharing a meal with them and use it as an opportunity to present the gospel. Giving cash might fund their addiction to alcohol or drugs. Be discerning with your kindness toward non-believers. Kind Christians give food, clothing and shelter in the name of Christ to point unbelievers to the true spiritual riches only He can give them (Matthew 6:31-33).

GROWING IN KINDNESS

First let's explore some hindrances to developing kindness in your life.

One roadblock to kindness is failing to deal with sin in your life. Ephesians 4:30-32 says, "Do not grieve the Holy Spirit of God, by whom you were sealed for the day of redemption. Let all bitterness and anger and wrath and shouting and slander be put away from you, along with all malice. Instead, be kind to one another, tender-hearted, graciously forgiving each other, just as God in Christ also has graciously forgiven you." When you allow sins like bitterness, anger and slander to go unchecked and unconfessed in your life, you grieve the Holy Spirit. You are not walking in the Spirit and are choosing instead to walk in the flesh. Here are some examples of what that looks like:

- Choosing to be controlled by your emotions
- Refusing to forgive
- Going to church for your needs to be met
- Focusing only on what is wrong in your life
- Blaming your spouse, job, church and family
- Forgetting to thank God for His blessings in your life

Whenever you are walking in the flesh, you are grieving the Spirit and are unable to display Christ's kindness.

Forgetting God's grace is another reason we fail to be kind to others. Remember the motive in Titus 2:11-12 for young women to live godly lives: "For the grace of God has appeared, bringing salvation to all men, instructing us that, denying ungodliness and worldly desires, we should live sensibly, righteously and godly in the present age." When you forget that you were lost and the great price that Christ paid for your salvation, you will stop being kind.

Like the Levite and the Priest in the parable of the Good Samaritan (Luke 10:25-37), you will walk right by the person in need when you forget that you too were once in desperate need. The kind Samaritan didn't walk by, and the kind Christian who deals with her sin and remembers God's grace, will not walk by either.

As you evaluate your kindness as a young woman, consider these three steps to growing into a kind person. Start with practicing, preparing and planning kindness.

First, random acts of kindness are nice, but to really see the power of kindness, start practicing intentional acts of kindness. They are far better and more powerful than you can imagine. Everyone knows someone who needs to be encouraged. Pick a sister in Christ, a family in crisis, or a child needing a solid example. Maybe this person came from a difficult family, a broken home, an unhealthy church, or an immoral background. Even though they are in Christ, they struggle with trusting God and battle with believing He is good.

Determine that each week, for three months, you will find a way to express kindness to this one specific person without fail. Send a note, give a gift, serve them, encourage them with well-chosen words, text Bible verses, ask for prayer requests and then pray. Be committed to showing kindness at least once a week for three months, then watch what God does.

Second, start preparing for a life of kindness. I remember ministering in India and being overwhelmed by the number of beggars and other deeply hurting people. I asked my missionary friend, "What do you do? How do you help them? How are you not overwhelmed with the need?" And he said, "You can't help everyone, but you can help some." Each day, my missionary friend was ready to help some of the needy around him. And you too need to be prepared to express kindness to those around you, in the name of Christ.

Being kind often requires preparation. Prepare for kindness by putting restaurant gift cards in your purse or wallet. Find those in your church who are out of work and bless them with a bag of surprise groceries. Seek out older widows who could use a visit from a cheerful young woman like yourself. When friends have a baby everyone else brings gifts, but you could serve them by bringing a meal, watching their kids, or picking up anything they need. Take the necessary steps by planning ahead to express kindness.

Third, start planning to show kindness in ways that are out of your comfort zone. Stretch your faith and demonstrate the love of Christ through you by:

- Asking the Lord to help you practice; prepare and plan to be kind.
- Giving money anonymously to someone at your church in need.
- Sharing things you already own with someone in need.
- Speaking and writing kind words to those who need some encouragement—not flattery, but truthful praise to another.
- Showing kindness through acts of service whether it's to individuals or your church family.
- Displaying kindness to people you see every week. Bring cookies to church fellowship, pass out stickers to young kids, thank your church leaders for their faithful service.
- Looking for those in the church who faithfully serve under the radar and express a kindness to them through a note or gift card.

Talk with your older women mentors about ways they express kindness and how they believe you can demonstrate kindness. Always give God the glory for what He does in you and through you. Remember Christ's great love and sacrifice for you on the Cross. Your response to His greatest act of love should be kindness toward others.

FOR PERSONAL REFLECTION & GROUP DISCUSSION:

1. Why do you think kindness is so important for a godly woman?

2. What is one of the greatest acts of kindness someone displayed to you?

3. What criteria and discernment do you need to determine which people to help and which ones you cannot?

4. How do you prepare your heart to show kindness so that you are ready when the need arises?

5. Write a list of all the ways the Lord has shown kindness to you. Pick two off your list and show the same type of kindness toward others.

10

LET THE WOMEN BE SUBMISSIVE

SUBJECT TO HER HUSBAND

"But I want you to understand that Christ is the head of every man, and the man is the head of a woman, and God is the head of Christ."

1 CORINTHIANS 11:3

Times sure have changed. Think about the way people used to travel. I found the following rules for riding in a stagecoach in *Uncle John's Bathroom Reader*:

1. If ladies are present, gentlemen are urged to forego smoking cigars and pipes as the odor of same is repugnant to the gentle sex. Chewing tobacco is permitted, but spit with the wind, not against it.
2. Don't snore loudly while sleeping or use your fellow passenger's shoulder for a pillow; he (or she) may not understand and friction may result.
3. Firearms may be kept on your person for use in emergencies. Do not fire them for pleasure or shoot at wild animals, as the sound riles the horses.

4. Gents guilty of unchivalrous behavior toward lady passengers will be put off the stage. It's a long walk back.
5. Abstinence from liquor is requested, but if you must drink, share the bottle. To do otherwise would make you appear selfish and un-neighborly.

These rules may seem outdated and humorous today but they were important to people over 100 years ago. Over time, rules can be altered when there are changes in morals, values or culture. We need to remember that biblical truth never changes with trends or advancements in society.

A TIMELESS TRUTH

The goal of every true Christian is to determine God's will and obey it even if churches, pastors and churchgoers don't practice or believe it. What's important is not what the internet or psychologists say, but what the Bible says. God is our Creator and Lord. Man in rebellion disagrees with God, but a Christian willingly submits to their Lord.

Today, many professing Christians live according to cultural values and preferences, while biblical truth is treated as optional. This danger can be clearly identified in people's attitudes toward the biblical design of a wife and mother.

It is important to learn and live what God's Word says regardless of the culture, society or time period. Learn to recognize what are preferences, the opinions of the majority and current trends of thought and compare them to the Scripture. For the born again Christian, the Word of God will be the authority over every opinion (including mine), any trend or cultural expression. The Bible is the absolute authority in any time and any place.

WE ALL HAVE TO SUBMIT

In chapter one of Titus, we learn that Paul left Titus on Crete to bring order to the church. That meant appointing qualified elders who would teach the Word of God and protect the church from error.

At the beginning of chapter two Paul tells Titus to mentor the church in healthy doctrine. What is healthy doctrine? It starts with an accurate interpretation of Scripture and then we submit our lives to the truth. A fruitful Christian life always begins with healthy doctrine.

You must submit to Christ in order to be right with God, then you live according to the Word of God in submission to the Holy Spirit. Titus 2 clearly and repeatedly tells us our motivation should be to willingly live in submission to God.

A primary reason to live this way is because of the grace of God. Because of what Jesus Christ has done for you and continues to do in you there is a desire to yield and follow Him. Titus 2:11-12 says, "For the grace of God has appeared, bringing salvation to all men, instructing us that, denying ungodliness and worldly desires, we should live sensibly, righteously and godly in the present age." God's grace instructs us how to live uniquely for Christ in a way that is radically different from the world.

Another reason you live this way is for your testimony. Titus 2:5 says, "Being subject to their own husbands, so that the word of God will not be slandered." Verse 8 states, "Sound in word which is irreproachable, so that the opponent will be put to shame, having nothing bad to say about us." Verse 10 declares, "Not pilfering, but demonstrating all good faith so that they will adorn the doctrine of God our Savior in everything." Having these qualities makes our lives an effective witness for God's truth.

The apostle says that young women are to "be subject to their own husbands, so that the Word of God will not be slandered." The enemy has done a very effective job of obscuring and perverting the truth of submission—not only in relation to a wife in marriage, but also to all God-appointed authority. Our society views submission as an outdated cultural expression that we are all finally free from. Yet in God's design, submission is a blessing because it brings structure, order and protection.

A BLESSING IN DISGUISE

The average woman can become hostile at the mere mention of the word submission. It is completely understandable when you consider the abuses and erroneous ideas about submission from both the world and the church. Add to that the failure of so many men to fulfill their God-designed role as a spiritual servant-leader, and you begin to understand why many women resent this word.

But don't forget that biblical submission is a good and godly quality. God's design for humanity involves submission in nearly every aspect of life. The Bible teaches submission in the following situations:

- To parents (Luke 2:51)
- To employers (Titus 2:9)
- To secular authorities (1 Peter 2:13)
- To law enforcement officials (Romans 13:1)
- To your church eldership (1 Peter 5:5)
- To God (James 4:7)
- To Christ (Ephesians 5:24)
- To the Word of God (Romans 8:7)

In addition to all those relationships, wives are specifically commanded to submit themselves to their own husbands. The submission of a wife to her husband is discussed five times in the New Testament. The opposite of submission is rebellion, a satanic attribute that must be put to death in the life of a true Christian.

Are you a submissive person? When your boss says do something, do you obey or resist? When your parents tell you they want you home by 11:00 p.m., do you try to comply or see how far you can stretch the limit? If you're married, when your husband asks you to do something, do you resist, ignore, backtalk, or do it with a heart of delight? When you make a mistake, do you make excuses or do you apologize from the heart? Do you find yourself making fun of your husband or do you honor him?

When you came to Christ, did you come to Him with a willing, tender, trusting, dependent heart? Or did you come to Christ with an independent, I'll-see-if-this-works-for-me mentality? If it was the second, you actually didn't come to Christ at all. And if you did come to Christ in the right way initially, are you truly a submissive person now? This is not easy for any of us to answer truthfully, but it is a question we should be asking repeatedly. Submission comes down to walking in the Spirit and at times there will be a battle with our flesh.

THE TRINITY AS A MODEL OF SUBMISSION

One of the great wonders of the Christian life is that the answers to all of life's questions are found in the character of God. When we understand who He is, we can better understand who we are, since He made us in His image.

The Trinity is a truth about God that helps us comprehend God's design for marriage, family, and relationships. The Trinity is the most glorious relationship that has or will ever exist. The divine relationship between the three persons of the Godhead gives us a model for husbands and wives, and a model for all relationships. Let's look at our God for a moment and worship Him. It is from the Trinity where we learn the absolute necessity of submission.

"The Trinity" is a term that defines the relationship of the Father, Son and Holy Spirit—one in essence and attributes, yet three in distinct work and purpose. Deuteronomy 6:4 says that "Yahweh is our God, Yahweh is one." Yet throughout the Old Testament, the Bible uses plural words—plural pronouns and verbs—to teach us that our God is a Trinity. The creation account says, "Let us make man in our image." In Isaiah 48:16 the coming Messiah, Jesus Christ, is speaking, and He says, "So now the Lord Yahweh has sent Me, and His Spirit." That verse refers to all three Persons of the Godhead separately.

At the very beginning of Jesus' earthly ministry, we witness the three Persons all manifested at one time. Matthew 3:16-17 says, "And after being baptized, Jesus came up immediately from the water; and behold, the heavens were opened, and he saw the Spirit of God descending like a dove and coming upon Him, and behold, there was a voice out of the heavens saying, 'This is My beloved Son, in whom I am well-pleased.'" In that passage you see all three Persons of the Trinity being the one God, yet each distinct in Person and function. They relate to One another and speak about each Other.

Matthew 28:19 says, "Go therefore and make disciples of all the nations, baptizing them in the name of the Father and the Son and the Holy Spirit." 2 Corinthians 13:14 says, "The grace of the Lord Jesus Christ, and the love of God, and the fellowship of the Holy Spirit, be with you all." The Trinity is a mystery that is evidence of the greatness of our God. He is greater than we can imagine. The God we love is one God, yet He exists in three distinct Persons or Personalities. It is amazing to study the Scriptures and find that within the unity and equality of the Godhead, there are different functions:

- 1 John 4:10 says the Father sent the Son.
- John 14:26 says the Father sends the Holy Spirit.
- John 15:26 says the Son and the Father send the Spirit.
- The prayer of Jesus in John 17 demonstrates the submission of Jesus the Son to God the Father.

"In the Trinity there is both a plurality and a unity, a perfect oneness. After the incarnation, there is clearly authority and submission."

In the Trinity there is both a plurality and a unity, a perfect oneness. After the incarnation, there is clearly authority and submission. All three Persons of the Trinity are equal, all three are God. They share the same essence, and yet there is submission and authority. Father, Son, Holy Spirit—not inferiority, not dominance, not dictatorship, but authority and submission nonetheless.

God uses that aspect of the Trinity to teach us how marriage is to work. This is the truth of 1 Corinthians 11:3: "I want you to understand that Christ is the head of every man, and the man is the head of a woman, and God is the head of Christ." As Paul is about to discuss the role of women, He makes this statement about the Trinity as the reason for different roles in marriage.

The principle of authority and submission in marriage is not archaic, cultural or outdated. Authority and submission are qualities found in the very Person and character of the unchanging God of the universe. Submission of a woman to her husband in marriage is not something men dreamed up. The principle and practice of submission has been around as long as God has existed. God is one and yet three. Likewise, in a Christian marriage, a couple is one and yet three (husband, wife and Christ).

To say that a wife's submission to her husband is demeaning would be to say that Christ's submission to the Father is also flawed. Christ's submission to the Father doesn't make him less than the Father. He is equal to the Father, but in God's design, the Son submitted to the Father. And if Christ's submission to the Father is not demeaning, neither is a wife to her husband.

DEFINING SUBMISSION

What does "be subject" mean? The Greek word from which it is translated, hupotasso, was used primarily as a military term. It comes from two words: hupo, meaning "under," and tasso, meaning "to arrange." So it means to rank or arrange under. The picture is one of a soldier who is under the authority of his commander, following his lead. This teaches us that submission has nothing to do with the worth or quality of a person, but only with authority and obedience:

- A nurse may be a more patient and kind person than a doctor, but she does not have the authority of a doctor.
- A child may live more morally than a parent, but she does not have the God-given authority of a parent.
- A wife may be more godly than her husband, but she does not have the authority God assigned to her husband.

Submission simply means to follow the lead of another. The wife is instructed to submit to her own husband. The word "submit" is used 39 times in the New Testament, with five of those directed specifically to wives, instructing them to submit to their own husbands. But the Bible never instructs all women to submit to all men.

Notice the language of God's instruction for wives concerning submission: "Wives, be subject to your own husbands, as to the Lord" (Ephesians 5:22); "Wives, be subject to your husbands, as is fitting in the Lord" (Colossians 3:18); "In the same way, you wives, be subject to your own husbands" (1 Peter 3:1); "For in this way in former times the holy women also, who hoped in God, used to adorn themselves, being subject to their own husbands" (1 Peter 3:5); "Being subject to their own husbands, so that the word of God will not be slandered" (Titus 2:5).

SUBMISSION IS A CHOICE

Each of those passages makes it clear that the submission of a wife is only to her own husband, not to every man. But also notice that this submission is voluntary. In all five New Testament passages, the Greek verbs are in the middle voice. That means the action of submission is personal choice. The wife submits herself, no one forces her to submit.

A woman chooses to practice submission for the glory of God. After prayer and discussion, a godly husband may have to request his bride to submit to his decision. In a crisis, husbands may give a gentle reminder to wives that they need to trust their spiritual leadership. But godly men never use submission as a tool for control. There is no command in the Bible instructing men to order their wives to submit. Instead husbands are commanded to love their wives, just as Christ also loves the church and gave Himself up for her (Ephesians 5:25).

"God's plan does not define what either of you should expect to get from marriage. Rather God's plan is for both the husband and wife to give to one another."

The husband is instructed to be the initiator of showing love, sharing God's perspective and seeking to obey God's Word. Do you realize what this does for a marriage? The husband dies to his will to serve his wife, and the wife dies to her will to submit to her husband. God's plan does not define what either of you should expect to get from marriage. Rather God's plan is for both the husband and wife to give to one another.

In Titus 2:5 Paul says that the wife is to subject herself to her own husband—why? "So that the Word of God will not be slandered." When we choose not to pursue submission we cause others to question the validity of the Word of God. When a Christian wife will not subject herself to her husband, she is dishonoring the Word of God.

God's design for women is not a culturally relative plan linked only to the first century. Submission is tied to God's eternal Word, which never changes; it is a part of His eternal design. Isaiah 40:8 reminds us, "The grass withers, the flower fades, but the word of our God stands forever." Refusing to submit is disobeying God's unchanging eternal standard.

When a woman refuses to submit herself to her husband as head, a myriad of consequences can result from this sinful choice. Submission is not a command of the husband, submission is a command from the Lord. It shows the world who our Master is. Wives, are you making it easy or difficult for your husband to fulfill his role of spiritual leadership? Has the Bible convinced you?

THE PRACTICE OF SUBMISSION

No woman becomes an incredible wife the moment she says, "I do." You have to prepare. If you are a young married woman or a single woman who is looking forward to marriage, now is the time to practice the principles of submission in your life. Here are some examples:

WALK AND TALK

1 Peter 3:1 says, "You wives, be subject to your own husbands so that even if any of them are disobedient to the word, they may be won without a word by the conduct of their wives." This verse says that it is possible for a Christian woman to win her husband to Christ.

Submission is shown by walking, not talking. You don't win him through confrontation or cramming the Bible down his throat. A wife shares Christ with a non-Christian husband when she lives in submission to him as unto the Lord. Her submission is proof positive of God's supernatural work in her heart.

A submissive wife doesn't nag or badger her husband. Submission is primarily shown in attitude and behavior. Why does a wife submit to an unsaved husband? She trusts God and therefore does not live in rebellion to Him or her husband. She believes in

God's design for marriage. She is a witness to a husband who is in rebellion to God, knowing that by her submission, she may win him.

1 Peter 3:2 says this can happen "as they observe your pure conduct with fear." Proverbs 31 further explains what such "pure conduct" is like when it tells us that a wife's godly behavior includes being trustworthy, supportive, productive, sacrificial, enterprising, hard-working and wise. This is not a picture of inferiority, weakness or inequality, but a picture of incredible spiritual strength.

"The wife who is biblically submissive is motivated by her love for Christ."

The wife who is biblically submissive is motivated by her love for Christ. Ephesians 5:22 says, "Wives, be subject to your own husbands, as to the Lord." Literally this means wives should submit to husbands as if their husband was the Lord Jesus Christ. Wow! "But he's not," you might say, "and I can't." That's right, but Jesus can through you. As you submit to Christ, the Holy Spirit enables you to submit to your husband. Jesus says, "Submit to him as you do to Me!"

The Bible refines submission further with special qualifications and clarifications:

Submission doesn't mean a woman should not express her feelings or opinions. When you are married you become one—like the perfect oneness found in the Trinity. For a husband and wife not to discuss or come to agreement about family matters is foolish. Whether dealing with issues of major importance like raising kids or less important ones like family vacations, talk it through together and seek to be of one mind. In some situations when there is disagreement, the godly wife will ultimately yield to her husband's leadership and support his decision.

Submission doesn't mean the wife should indulge in sin. The Word of God teaches submission to authority, unless the one in authority demands that you disobey God. At that point, you must submit to God's authority rather than the human authority. You obey and honor your government, pay your taxes, and fulfill your duties as citizens unless the government orders you to disobey God. At that point, you must obey God rather than men. The same is true in marriage. You should obey your husband except when he demands that you sin. But even then, your obedience to God should be expressed with the humble heart of Christ toward your husband.

Submission doesn't mean allowing abuse in the marriage. Women should seek help from church and legal authorities if abuse occurs and should remove themselves from any dangerous situations until changes are made. Proverbs 22:3 and 27:12 say that "a prudent man sees evil and hides."

HEART AND ACTIONS

Understand that submission begins with an internal heart attitude. Look at 1 Peter 3:3-4, "Your adornment must not be merely external—braiding the hair, and wearing gold jewelry, or putting on garments; but let it be the hidden person of the heart, with the incorruptible quality of a lowly and quiet spirit, which is precious in the sight of God."

The godly wife pursues submission in her heart attitude as well as her behavior. She gives her whole heart to her husband in a strong but gentle way, exercising great wisdom in her choice of words. Her greatest attractiveness is not external, but internal, with a positive attitude and a focus on serving others. When she's been hurt, instead of pulling back to protect herself, she gives her heart again to the Lord. As a result, she maintains a submissive heart toward her husband.

Submission includes speaking respectful and complimentary words, encouraging and building up your husband, motivating him to be the best husband he can be, and expecting him to be the leader he is supposed to be. Men need a sense of significance—that's why Ephesians 5:33 says wives are to respect their husbands.

WHAT NOT TO SAY

In addition to not saying too much to your husband (because you can win him "without a word"), there are some things you should never say:

Don't say, "I just can't do it." If you are thinking this way, you're partially correct. You can't do it unless you are filled with the Spirit. Christians have all of the Spirit (indwelt). But does He have all of you (filled)? On your own, you don't have the resources to submit to your husband. But empowered by the Holy Spirit, you have the ability to be Christlike.

A fulfilling marriage and a godly family are primarily the results of pursuing a closer walk with Christ, not merely from trying to be nice to your husband and kids. It's like a triangle—the closer you move to Christ at the top, the closer together you and your husband will become.

As you pursue Christ, He will help you be submissive, which will benefit your marriage and family and bring glory to God.

Don't say, "He'll never be the spiritual leader." Prayer is powerful. God's promises are powerful. Living by faith in obedience to the Word of God is powerful. Stop trying to change your husband, and let God change you. An on-fire, submissive, Spirit-filled prayer warrior is a powerful change agent in the hands of the living God. Strive to be that woman.

Don't say, "Submission is not for me." It doesn't matter if you're married or not—all the qualities in Titus 2 and Proverbs 31 are the same. Study the two passages and you will see their similarities. The role of women is the same in the Old Testament and the New Testament and it is the same today. God is consistent and His design has not changed.

As a single woman, learn to submit yourself to authority. Submit to your parents, government and church leaders, so one day you'll be ready to submit to your husband. The issue is not the person to whom you submit, but your heart's willingness.

PERSONAL TESTIMONY

As a conclusion to this book, let me encourage you by sharing the story of one single Christian woman. She was born again at the age of 20. She came from parents who were drunks and divorced when she was a teenager. Her dad lived with his girlfriend, and her mom married and divorced three times, each husband also being a drunkard. She had some religious exposure to Catholicism but was cast adrift to find her own way. Her teenage years were rough and the consequences of a party lifestyle helped her to see her own sin. When invited by some distant relatives to visit a church, she responded to the gospel message and was born again. In God's providence, her work forced her to move and her previous church leaders recommended that she attend Grace Community Church under the teaching ministry of John MacArthur. She didn't understand the Bible very well yet, but she had a new heart that hungered for it.

She bought tabs for her Bible so she could keep up with the preacher. She got invited to the college ministry by a gal she never saw again after that initial invitation. In her heart, she committed to go even if she didn't know anyone, because she knew she needed fellowship. While continuing to work at various jobs, she also began to attend college Bible studies, was discipled by older women, and soon afterward began to serve in the junior high ministry. There she met some additional young married couples and families with small children and began to witness something she had never seen before: a biblical family. She met husbands who adored and cherished their wives, loved their kids, and humbly and graciously led their families with Christlike servant-hearts.

She saw women submit to their husbands, not because they were told to, but because they wanted to.

There was a oneness in these marriages she had never seen. There was a commitment to love, cherish and serve each other. And there was joy, romance and a union that seemed supernatural. In her heart, she began to pursue those very things as a single. She became a friend and babysitter to these couples and young families. She enjoyed watching how they functioned and asked them pointed questions. She began to grow and mature as a woman of God and slowly became a leader among young women on the junior high ministry staff. She began to have a reputation as an amazing single woman of God who pursued undistracted devotion to her Lord.

I actually heard about this woman before I ever met her. The godliest older men in my life—my mentors, both married and single—would speak of her in hushed tones because of her genuine commitment to Christ. There was amazing respect for her example and her ministry. She herself began to think that maybe she was set apart to be the wife of a pastor if marriage was in her future.

When I met this gal (named Jean Sharpe) for the first time, it was somewhat anticlimactic. She had been built up in my mind from all the incredible comments everyone else made about her. I had not met her but when I did, I discovered that she actually did leave footprints when she walked, rather than floating above the ground like I thought she would from what I had heard about her.

She was sort of dating my roommate. My roomie was a godly guy and when they determined to not pursue their relationship any further, he looked at me, and said, "You know Chris, you and Jean might be perfect for each other." I filed that comment away.

After over a year of being friends with each other, things progressed in our relationship to the point where I asked my mentor what he thought about me dating Jean and his reaction was classic. He rolled back in his chair, laughed out loud and said,

"What took you so long?" We were married a year later. As I write this, that is now 40 years ago.

In our 40-year marriage, Jean and I have rarely talked about the roles of men and women as a couple. We have rarely talked about the submission of wives or the leadership of husbands. We are both committed to live our lives seeking to be filled with the Spirit. We also honor the Bible as our authority and try to live obediently to His Word in every area of our lives. Of course we are not perfect, but our goal is to be obedient in all things. We seek to live out what God says about marriage and His design for men and women, and it works. We are one heart and one mind and we function in our roles and as a result God has blessed us incredibly. We have had fights, disagreements and arguments—some were painful and difficult. But in that, we also know the joy of repentance and forgiveness. As we both look back at the four decades of marriage, filled with so many blessings, joys and sweet memories, we are overwhelmed by God's graciousness to us. We have an amazing marriage and enjoy being best friends for life.

Jean remained a stay-at-home mom to our two boys. She is a homemaker. She worked for a year as a part of the children's ministry of our church when our two boys were in late high school and college, not because it was necessary but because it was a way for Jean to serve Christ even more. Not surprisingly, both our sons are married to homemakers—amazingly gifted and treasured daughters-in-law. Both our boys married women who were determined to be stay-at-home moms, not because we told them to do that but because they saw what a difference that commitment makes in a marriage and the lives of children. They married women who seek to live out the character qualities of Titus 2 because they had a mom who lived those qualities in front of them for years. So far, we are blessed now with three grandsons and are already praying for their future wives, knowing what an amazing difference marriage to a Titus 2 woman can make.

My bride came from a rough background, but because of God's

grace and the timeless truths you have read about in this book, she and I have enjoyed many great blessings. I hope and pray you do as well.

God's Word holds women in high esteem and God's design for women is perfect in every way—may this book free you to pursue God's will by God's Word through God's Spirit to God's glory.

FOR PERSONAL REFLECTION & GROUP DISCUSSION:

1. Why do you think submission is so important to God?

2. What are some good examples of submission that you have personally witnessed?

3. How can you grow and develop submission in your heart?

4. What counsel would you give to a woman who says, “Submission is unfair”?

5. Look at the life of Jesus in the Gospels. What can we learn from His submission to God and others?

A SUMMARY FOR SINGLE WOMEN

Singleness can be one of the most difficult seasons for a Christian woman. Young women in the first century avoided the difficulties of singleness by marriage arrangements that happened even as young as age twelve. In the 21st century the single season for a Christian woman can be massively challenging. Yet, we know any believer seeking to obey God's Word through the Holy Spirit can pursue His design and be prepared for a life that glorifies God whether single or married. To do so she needs to understand her singleness and what God might have in store for her future. Her relationship to Christ, parents, friends, church, schooling and career all need to be shaped by Scripture in order to grow into a Titus 2 and Proverbs 31 woman.

FOUNDATIONAL PRINCIPLES

Men and women are equal before God, yet have different roles and responsibilities. Both are equally responsible to glorify God individually as their highest priority, as well as keep Him central in every aspect of life.

Except for the celibate, the most fulfilling God-given role for a woman is that of a wife and mother. For a godly man, the most fulfilling role is that of a husband and father, not a career. A career is designed to provide for a family and to be a witness for Christ. A career was never designed to be the focus and priority of anyone's life. Our identity in Christ, our commitment to the church, representing Christ to the lost and the hope of heaven are far more important than a career.

If a single woman believes she is to remain celibate (never to marry), she should know what God says about celibacy. Matthew 19:12 addresses eunuchs, however the same principles of celibacy can apply to women.

- Congenital reasons (born a celibate physically)
- Physical reasons (made a celibate physically)
- Commitment to God (choosing to have no sexual relations though capable of such).

Concerning a commitment to celibacy 1 Corinthians 7:1-9, says: First, celibacy is good (verse 1). It has advantages for the kingdom and for God's purposes. A single woman is freer to serve Christ because she is unhindered by a husband or children. Second, maintaining celibacy requires self-control (verse 9). Celibacy makes one vulnerable to lustful temptation, especially if God did not create you to be celibate. Third, celibacy is a gift from God (verse 7). The Bible indicates celibacy is only for a few, according to the sovereign plan of God. Celibacy definitely doesn't make one more spiritual, but the purpose of celibacy is greater sacrifice for the kingdom.

For a single Christian woman to be celibate, all four of the following statements should be true:

1. She is content in her singleness.
2. She experiences no physical sexual temptation that leads her to sin.
3. She has the heart to give herself completely and selflessly to ministry.
4. Providentially, God has not provided a godly suitor.

THE CHALLENGE OF SINGLENESS

If a single born again woman in our culture today is not celibate, she will find herself in a state of tension until marriage because of four reasons:

1. **A gap in time.** In biblical times most young women went from being under her father's authority to a husband, with no period in between. She never left home, was not independent, never had a career, but simply transitioned from living with her parents to living with her husband.

Today there is commonly a gap in time between growing up at home, then getting married and starting a family. That time gap is often filled with education, a career and even ministry.

2. **No modeling.** Most of today's single Christian women have not witnessed older women modeling biblical principles. When I last conducted a survey, less than 10% of women said their mom and dad truly lived out the biblical pattern of women's and men's roles in their marriage.
3. **No specific time frame.** The single woman cannot know when being a wife and mother will become a reality. During this time of singleness there are challenging questions about what she should be doing until marriage. Should she pursue a career, a graduate degree, greater involvement in ministry, or become a missionary? Will she make money to spend on herself, to appear successful or will she prepare to be a wife and mother?
4. **Wordly pressure.** Our society pressures young women to find her significance outside the family and home. She is encouraged to make money, gain fame, advance in a career, be independent, assert herself and take control. There is little thought of how these ideals are inconsistent with God's design for women.

SOLUTIONS TO THE CHALLENGE

What can she do as she lives on her own, when the potential of being married and having children seems a distant dream? Here are three responses springing from the Scripture alone:

DO ALL TO THE GLORY OF GOD

1 Corinthians 10:31 says, "Whether, then, you eat or drink or whatever you do, do all to the glory of God." You start living for the glory of God by making sure you evaluate your motives for

everything you pursue. Are you living for His glory or for your desires?

Ask the Lord to help you determine the motive behind going to school. Is it for self, pride, a degree, fame or is it for evangelism, edification, personal growth, worship and the development of life skills?

Ask the Lord to help you determine why you are pursuing a job or career. Is it because of the pressure to please others, to gain money to buy things you want and tell others what to do, or are you working to evangelize the lost, be edified, worship Christ and develop skills to serve His purposes?

Ask the Lord to help you determine why you are serving in ministry. Is it for fame, the esteem of others or to feel important? Is it out of self-sacrificing love for Christ or to use your spiritual gifts within the church?

BE THANKFUL FOR YOUR GOD-GIVEN ROLE AS A WOMAN

Whether you are celibate or not, honor the role of wife, mother and homemaker in attitude, action and word. As a Christian, you should desire to esteem that which God esteems, to praise what He praises, to honor what He honors. The Lord treasures His design for a wife, mother, and homemaker. Proverbs 31:10 says, "An excellent wife, who can find? For her worth is far above pearls," and 31:30 says, "Charm is deceitful and beauty is vain, but a woman who fears Yahweh, she shall be praised."

Be thankful for singleness as a time to minister unhindered by family responsibilities while looking forward to marriage. Paul says the purpose of singleness is "to promote propriety and undistracted devotion to the Lord" (1 Corinthians 7:35). The most important question to ask yourself is this; "Am I acting appropriately and pursuing undistracted devotion to the Lord?"

BE A RESPONSIBLE CHRISTIAN WITH A STRONG FAITH NOW

Again, the crucial commitment to pursuing God's design for

women is to begin that journey now as a young single. Single Christian women need to prepare for the role of a wife, mother, and homemaker by studying and practicing the scriptural principles that apply to those roles. They should also learn the skills of Bible study, prayer, ministry, discipleship, budgeting, cleaning, organizing, nutrition, managing emotions and much more.

A single Christian woman needs to also understand that her present ministry (church, school, career, missions) will one day transition to her future ministry (marriage, family and home). Developing this understanding and anticipating this change will allow the young single woman to be at a huge advantage.

She also needs to learn how to maintain proper relationships with her parents, spiritual mentors and leaders in her church. Learning from those who are ahead of you in life helps to avoid pitfalls and produces wisdom.

Developing friendships with Spirit-filled men-of-character is something she should be open to. As she develops relationships, she should always maintain biblical convictions and seek to please the Lord. In this way God may allow the relationship to grow and develop into something more.

Young women who want to be Christlike should continue to develop all the qualities for young women as described in Titus 2:4-5 and seek the mentoring of older godly women as described in Titus 2:3. Along with those relationships, they should also seek to be mentored by godly couples, with and without children, and to manifest a heart of submission to the authorities God has placed in their lives.

In closing, the single young Christian woman should believe the promises in Psalm 84:11:

Yahweh God is a sun and shield;
Yahweh gives grace and glory;
No good thing does He withhold
from those who walk blamelessly.

God's Plan of Salvation

Everyone is destined to die, but life does not end with death. The Bible says that after death there will be a judgment where each person will give an account of his life to God (Hebrews 9:27). When God created Adam and Eve in His own image in the garden of Eden, He gave them an abundant life, and the freedom to choose between good and evil. They chose to disobey God and go their own way. As a consequence, death was introduced into the human race, not only physical death, but also spiritual death. For this reason, all human beings are separated from God.

Unfortunately, man's fallen nature and his on-going choices to sin, results in men living in continual disobedience to God: *for all have sinned and fall short of the glory of God (Romans 3:23)*. This is humanity's problem: because of sin everyone is separated from God (Isaiah 59:2).

People have tried to overcome this separation in many ways: by doing good, by practicing religion or creating their own ideas of salvation, or by attempting to live a good, moral and fair life. However, none of these things is enough to cross the barrier of separation between God and humanity, because God is holy and human beings are sinful. Regardless of how good you think you are, each and every human being has lied, stolen, been angry, lusted, hated, hurt others, resisted God and defied His perfect character.

This spiritual separation has become the condition of mankind, and because of this they are condemned: *He who believes in Him is not judged; he who does not believe has been judged already, because he has not believed in the name of the only begotten Son of God (John 3:18).*

God's Love and Plan

Jesus Christ said:

> *For God so loved the world, that He gave His only begotten Son, that whoever believes in Him shall not perish, but have eternal life (John 3:16).*
>
> *I came that they may have life, and have it abundantly (John 10:10).*
>
> *He who believes in the Son has eternal life; but he who does not obey the Son will not see life, but the wrath of God abides on him (John 3:36).*
>
> *I am the way, and the truth, and the life. No one comes to the Father but through Me (John 14:6).*

God's holiness makes it impossible for Him to relate to sinful humanity, and His justice demands that every sinner be judged and condemned to an eternal separation from God. Because of this, all people have become enemies of God. Although God has every right to condemn every single person, because of His love He provided a solution through His Son, Jesus Christ. God knew people could not save themselves, so God determined to save sinners. God sent His Son, Jesus Christ, 100% God and 100% man, to bear the sins of His children on the cross. Jesus' death was the only acceptable sacrifice for sin: *And there is salvation in no one else, for there is no other name under heaven that has been given among men by which we must be saved (Acts 4:12).*

When Jesus died on the cross, He paid the penalty for the sins of His children—the penalty which was death—and thereby established a bridge between God and people. Anyone who puts their trust in Christ can be saved. Because of this sacrifice, every person who is born again can have true fellowship with God now and forever.

Jesus Christ Is Alive Today

After Jesus Christ died on the cross at Calvary, where He received the punishment that we deserved, the Bible says that He was buried in a tomb. But He did not remain there: Christ rose from the dead! For all those who believe in Jesus Christ, His resurrection is a guarantee that they will also be resurrected to eternal life in the presence of God forever. This is very good news! *Christ died for our sins...was buried, and...He was raised on the third day according to the Scriptures (1 Corinthians 15:3-4).*

How to Receive God's Love and Plan

In His mercy, God has determined that salvation is free. To receive it, agree with and believe these four things:

1. Acknowledge your deadly problem. You are a sinner by nature, and you have chosen to sin repeatedly violating God's law and missing the mark of God's perfect character. Because you have sinned, you have missed God's perfect plan for you and you are separated now from God.
2. Repent, by turning from your hated sins, and put your faith in Christ by being completely dependent upon Christ, trusting in His Work on the cross to provide you with salvation, forgiveness of sins, abundant life now and eternal life forever.
3. Publicly acknowledge that Jesus Christ is God, who died, taking your place on the cross for your sins, then because He had no sin of His own, rose from the dead, ascended into heaven and is the only one who can make you right with God.
4. Then, from a new heart that wants to obey (Romans 6:17), get to know Christ by learning His Word, love Christ by treasuring His Word and follow Christ by obeying His Word.

The Bible says:

...that if you confess with your mouth Jesus as Lord, and believe in your heart that God raised Him from the dead, you will be saved (Romans 10:9).
...for "Whoever calls on the name of the Lord will be saved"(Romans 10:13).

A Prayer to Receive Jesus Christ

Cry out to Christ Jesus and beg Him to awaken your heart that is dead and your mind that is blind, and ask Him to give you a NEW HEART that can express faith in Him and repent from sin. Admit that you cannot save yourself; that no one but Christ can deliver you from sin. Acknowledge that Christ is God who alone can make you right with God now and forever because of His death on the cross and His resurrection from the dead.

When He saves you, you will look the same on the outside but you will not be the same on the inside. You will have a willingness to do whatever Christ wants (Luke 14). You will want to obey His Word (Romans 6:17), gather with His people and worship Him by offering your entire life to Him (Romans 12:2), follow Him in every aspect of life in order to know Christ more intimately as your first love (Revelation 2:7).